"Delilah is radio's equivalent to Oprah Winfrey. Delilah is appealing to the listener because her show is centered around relationships."

—*Chicago Tribune*

"Delilah wants every call to end on an 'audio hug' of empathy and recognition, and it does, it does. Inevitably she lifts us up where we belong."

—*New York Times*

"Whether the caller is celebrating a birthday. . .or grappling with tragedy, Delilah offers soothing words and musical commentary."

—*People*

"[Delilah] treats her listeners like they are friends gathered at her not-so-fancy kitchen table, sharing some soft-rock tunes, some tea and some stories."

—*San Jose Mercury News*

"On and off the air, she is the friendly next door neighbor with time to talk over a virtual backyard fence."

—*New York Times*

"Rather than trying to advise the callers or fix the situation, Delilah simply relates to the audience. Then, she matches the situation with music."

—*Radio Ink*

Delilah®

LOVE MATTERS

Remarkable Love Stories that Touch the
Heart and Nourish the Soul

HARLEQUIN®

HARLEQUIN®

LOVE MATTERS: Remarkable Love Stories That Touch the Heart and Nourish the Soul

ISBN-13: 978-0-373-89200-6
ISBN-10:   0-373-89200-4
© 2008 by Big Shoes Production, Inc.

This book contains materials from various contributors and the author of this book. Names and identifying characteristics of certain individuals have been changed in order to protect their privacy.

www.eHarlequin.com

Printed in U.S.A.

This book is dedicated to my Janey.

You are the wind beneath my wings.

Contents

Acknowledgments

This book is a creation that comes from the wonderful relationship I enjoy with my listeners. I am blessed to be on the radio for more than thirty years now, and love the experience in 2008 as much as I did in 1976 when I first found my way to a microphone at an AM radio station. Many years and many radio stations later, I am fortunate enough to be heard at night on some of the premier radio stations in North America, playing sappy love songs by incredible music artists and talking and writing with listeners all night long. There's not a night that goes by without one listener phone call that reminds me of why I love doing what I do as a profession. I cherish my relationship with the listeners, and this book reflects the way we communicate with each other. I thank each listener who chooses to participate with such a story, particularly those who are contributing to my first book published with Harlequin.

I wish to recognize the staff I love to laugh with and work with in the studio each night; without them it wouldn't be nearly as fun and it wouldn't be possible to connect with as many of you as I do each night. My thanks also goes to the program directors and general managers at the radio stations who choose to air me in the evenings, so that I might be heard by as many of you as possible. We try especially hard to please each and every radio station in North America that carries our program. My appreciation is also extended to the distributors of my radio program. In the United States, Premiere Radio Networks has a wonderful staff that creates these opportunities to connect. In Canada, the staff at Sound Source works diligently to create the same opportunities. Individual thanks go to my editor, Joan Marlow Golan, who has shown an amazing appreciation for the reader and the listener and believes in the power of Love in the same way I do. The staff of Harlequin Books receives my gratitude for the work they have done to create this series of books, starting with *Love Matters*, and to open so many opportunities for us to share these stories—they are gracious and highly competent. Thanks to Donna Trent, Nicole Keller and Maria Rivas for their contributions, as well as Scott Westgaard, Simona Salter, Jim Ryan, Brian Depoe, Eileen Thorgusen, Mike McVay, Bruce Hudson and Tom Drennon.

Introduction

There is only one happiness in life,
to love and be loved.

—GEORGE SAND

Why does love matter? I think it's really all that does. Everything else that matters, matters because of love. If a fire burns, it matters because someone or something we love might be hurt, even destroyed. If a birthday is celebrated, the celebration matters only if we are surrounded by those that we love. If a life is mourned, it is not mourned for what was accomplished nearly so much as for the love that will be missed.

If you listen to my nightly radio show, you know I refer to myself as the "Queen of Sappy Love Songs," so it seems natural that I would believe love matters, but what do I mean by love? Any attempt at defining—or maybe a better word is describing—what I think love is will fall short, but a feeble attempt is important as we indulge our hearts in a multitude of stories of love that matters.

A lot of people think love is an emotion—that uplifting feeling we carry in the core of our bodies when we are rushing headlong into a new relationship. When I was a teenager, and again as a young woman, I thought that each time I felt that surge of joy and energy in my chest (and other places farther south), I was experiencing "Love." It got to be such a joke with my girlfriends that my childhood pal Dee Dee had a T-shirt printed up with the message "It's for real this time," because each time I felt I was in love, I would declare with all the sincerity a seventeen-year-old girl can muster, "Really, this is the *real* thing, it is love this time. . . ." I still think the intoxicating high of romance, the dizzying experience of having your senses overwhelmed while falling in love, can be part of real love, but just a tiny part.

Some of the bead-wearing hippies I used to hang out with back in the day in Eugene, Oregon, explained to me that love was a force, an energy field that surrounds us with light. They told me that I could meditate, dance or chant to create more of this positive love energy swirling and flowing all around me. It seems to me that love is created by building relationships rather than by waving your hands over your head in a snakelike motion, the way my friends in tie-dyed shirts encouraged me to do as they listened to the music of Bob Marley and partook of herbal enlightenment. Still, I believe in the positive energy of love, which empowers and inspires all who love and are loved.

The more years I spend on this planet, the more I realize how very little I know about anything, and that includes relationships. I find it ironic that I host a radio show focused on relationships and love songs when I've been divorced three times and even now don't have all the answers to how to make relationships work and endure. Still, I feel I've learned a lot about love over the years, both from my own life experiences and from the touching love stories listeners confide in me when they phone in to my radio show every night or when they e-mail me.

One of the amazing things I have discovered these past few years, as I rethink all my previous beliefs and attitudes about relationships, is what a cruel disservice we do to young people when we impose on them "rules" of relationships that were once handed down to us. Among the "rules" I have had to unlearn is the belief that you can only love one person in your life. Or if you love one person and that relationship comes undone, you can't love another until you "stop" loving Person A. Or if you love Person B, then you certainly can't still be in love with Person A. Especially if Person A is a jerk or has abused your heart in any way. It may not seem reasonable to go on loving a person who is deficient in kindness or compassion or other admirable qualities, but as the philosopher Pascal famously said, "The heart has reasons that reason knows nothing of."

I think the reason my radio show has enjoyed such popularity is that when my listeners call in to request a song or share a dedication, they trust me with their heart. They let me "know" a bit about their situation, their dreams or their lovers. Despite the public forum, people feel safe allowing me to peek into the windows of their heart each and every night. It's a phenomenon that I don't understand and haven't seen with any of my radio host peers, but after just a four- or five-minute conversation with me, a complete stranger, listeners often share thoughts, feelings, secrets that they haven't felt comfortable sharing with those closest to them. Maybe the level of anonymity, given that I am merely a disconnected voice on the radio and they are calling from the privacy of their own home, without a face or a last name and perhaps even with a made-up first name, gives them the freedom to be transparent. The level of intimacy people feel toward me and my staff is a gift and an honor that I thank God for every day.

When callers let me into the innermost recesses of their hearts, I try to be very, very respectful. I won't ever air a call, no matter how juicy or compelling or funny or powerful, if the person who has opened their heart to me would be harmed or hurt in any way. For instance, one night a woman called me to dedicate a song to her "boyfriend"—the man she was having an affair with behind her husband's back. Her husband was a cop. Who carried a gun. Who was jealous. . . Needless to say, that call was never aired.

Former bosses have said to me about such callers, "They *know* they are going to be recorded and put on the air. Who cares if they got foolish and shared things they shouldn't have said—it's *great* radio!" But I care far less about ratings than about respect. I would not feel good about myself or my show if I ever exploited anyone. God did not elevate me to the position I am in to hurt others.

I play love songs every night, thousands of them over my career in radio. (I figured out the math one time—I play ten or eleven songs per hour, five hours a night. I've been doing this show for almost 24 years—that adds up to over 335,125 songs, not counting my weekend shows!) I know the lyrics to love songs from every decade since the 40s, when my parents started collecting records. I know the lyrics to silly love songs, tragic love songs and sex-you-up love songs (Oh, Barry White, sing to me. . .). Some of these songs make a mockery of love, and most touch upon just one aspect of love—romantic love. But many try to encompass the total nature and essence of love, and when the words of these songs marry the melody and cadence, the result is truly amazing. A young woman named Monica wrote and recorded a song called "For You I Will," and the lyrics touch upon what I think real love is, the kind of love that makes life worth living. When you love someone with the kind of love described in the lyrics of this song—when you love so much that you would be willing to put your life on the line, to fight, even die, for the one you love—then that's ultimate love, the kind God has for us.

I've read stories, in the newspaper and online, of soldiers fighting overseas who throw themselves on a grenade in order to save the lives of their comrades. In 2006 I sat in Landstuhl, the military hospital in Germany, holding the hands of young American servicemen and women—some just boys and girls—who had lost limbs and organs, fighting wars in the Middle East they didn't necessarily understand. What surprised me the most was the love their fellow soldiers displayed when they visited them. Oh, the tears that ran down those strained and weary faces, old before their time, as they held the hands of their wounded friends. And one after another wounded soldier told me, "I want to go back and be with my buddies."

I know I feel that way for my children and close family members, but as I grow in love, I realize there are other people God has brought into my life that I would also fight for, even die for. It amazes me when I try to understand that God loves all of us this much—that is a concept far too profound for me to comprehend. There are about a dozen people, outside of my children, to whom I would not hesitate to donate a major organ in order to save their lives, even if I still needed that organ. But the thought of giving up my life for a stranger, or a con artist who swindles people out of their hard-earned money, or a child molester who escapes justice or a man who beats his wife and kids. . .that is a type of love I will never be able to understand or emulate. I'm not that loving. I'm glad God is.

Although I'm no poster child for wedded bliss, my marriages did begin in love and had some special moments, and my relationships with family and friends have endured and taught me much about everlasting love. I've also learned to appreciate love because of the times I didn't feel I had enough of it. Many radio stations change "air personalities" as frequently as every eighteen months, and earlier in my career I had to relocate quite a bit. This led to some pretty lonely times, far away from loved ones, trying to cope as a single mom. And I've known the pain of losing love—the pain of being disowned by my dad and his family when, at age twenty-one, I married an African-American man; the pain of losing my brother Matt and his wife in a plane accident; the pain of being left by my first husband for another woman; the pain of multiple divorces and of having to tell my children that they would no longer live in a two-parent home.

It's love that's given me my mission in life, to be a voice for those who have no voice. I have spent my entire life being a "voice" on the air, sharing thoughts and words each night. And since 2003, I've tried to be the voice for the children born into destitution in a refugee camp at Buduburam, Ghana, that has been the main focus of my Point Hope Foundation. Point Hope also seeks to be the voice of thousands of children stuck in the foster care system in the United States.

With God's direction and inspiration, and the help and love of many others, I've been able to keep my promise to the mothers of Buduburam that I would find a way to get fresh water to their babies. After three years, a lot of frustration, and soooo much money I can't stand to think about it, fresh water is now in the camp. When the water started flowing, I cried with joy that God was able to give us the resources to follow through on that promise, and with gratitude for all the help from Kraig, Chris, Quasi and others, whose hard work and love made this a reality. Love will also bring to fruition other projects in the refugee camp—gardens, a chicken farm, a fish pond, a feeding program, education and much more. My dream is a healthy, loving community for every child.

In this book, I'll share more of my own love stories and reflections as well as some of the amazing love stories that listeners have e-mailed to me over the years. Many of the stories in *Love Matters* focus on romantic and married love, but because love starts in the family, I've started there, too, with stories of love for family and friends. Then the book moves on to stories about finding and cherishing true love; losing and then rediscovering love with the same person many years later; being given a second (or third or fourth) chance at love with someone new; and finally letting go of the ones we love, either because death has claimed them or because they're not part of our life's journey anymore. Just as I do on the air, I've chosen songs that suit each story and used the song title as the heading for each letter. I'm grateful to the listeners who've given us permission to share their stories about how love has changed their lives for the better, helping them to grow, to heal, to give and give back or pay forward, to find meaning and purpose and beauty in life, to bring them closer to God and to the people in their hearts and in their lives.

Love matters because when all else passes away, it

remains. The love that we shared with God, the love that we shared with our family and friends, our lovers and our neighbors, our co-workers and strangers who crossed our paths. As Saint Paul stated so eloquently in 1 Corinthians 13:13, "And now these three remain: faith, hope and love. But the greatest of these is love." The stories in this book reaffirm the truth of this, and I hope all who read them will be inspired to love someone, and someone else, and someone else. . . .

Love for Family and Friends

"In family life, love is the oil that eases friction,
the cement that binds closer together, and
the music that brings harmony."

—Eva Evelyn Burrows,
13th General of the Salvation Army

Family has been celebrated in numerous popular songs, e.g., the bouncy Sister Sledge anthem "We Are Family" and—my personal favorite—Carole King's "Child of Mine," and with reason, because the family is the foundation for all of our love relationships to come, good or bad. I believe if children have but *one* person in their world who loves them fiercely, they will survive. If they don't have the assurance that they matter from at least one adult, then they are broken for life. I was raised in a traditional "nuclear" family, the norm in our little town in Reedsport, Oregon. It wasn't until years after I left home that I discovered how "*un*-normal" our American concept of family—a mother, father, two kids and a dog—is in many other cultures. Elsewhere in the world families live in dwellings with multiple generations, extended family members and even, in some cultures, multiple wives. My children have never experienced a "normal" family atmosphere, with a mother and father and full siblings. But they have known that they have a mother who loves them fiercely, and they know that I will love them unconditionally all the days of their lives.

As a child, I learned to love from the best, my mom, Wilma. Whatever her shortcomings, she believed in all four of her children and made sure we believed in ourselves. Her encouragement created in me a solid core of self-confidence that has been invaluable to me in my career as a radio host. Mom was a big woman—she stood over six feet tall, and her arm span was that of a giant. And, oh, when she wrapped you in those strong arms, you *knew* you were loved!

Wilma showed her love in a million different ways—one was that she baked treats for her family. How we loved her cookies! Chocolate chip for the boys, oatmeal raisin for me and Dad, sugar cookies and applesauce with spice during the holidays. My parents both died within a few years of each other, each at the age of fifty-seven, and among the houseful of "stuff" that my siblings and I were left to sell or donate was a cookie jar. That cookie jar sat in Mom's kitchen for forty years and was rarely empty. Years later I walked into a thrift store and saw an identical cookie jar and started to cry, so I bought it and took it home. Not because I needed a new cookie jar, but because that ceramic jar reminded me of the hot cookies my mom would bake for us every week and the way she would ask, "Sis, you want to help me bake cookies?" This question was really an invitation to stand in our tiny kitchen and spend time laughing and talking to Mom about my friends, my homework, my latest crush, my future dreams. As we made cookies together, my mom and I bonded in love.

I also learned a lot about love from my father. It is only now, as my own children are growing at the speed of light, that his lessons are resounding in my heart. He was a stoic man, not one to hug and kiss and gush like Mom, but he showed his love through his steadfast commitment to his family. When the toaster broke, he would stay up all night to repair it, so we could have toast with our eggs in the morning. When the holidays rolled around, he disappeared into the garage, his makeshift Santa's workshop, to build toys and wooden objects for everyone in our neighborhood.

Although our parents give us our first lessons in love, perhaps our best teachers about love are our kids. The greatest joy of love in my life has been in giving birth to three wonderful children and adopting seven more. When I held my firstborn, Isaiah, I knew that my life would never be the same. For the rest of my natural life, my heart would be walking around outside my body, in the form of my child. I learned more about love from Isaiah in the first few hours of his life than I had learned in the twenty-four years of my life prior to nursing him to my breast. For eight years Isaiah and I were alone, just the two of us, going camping and dirt biking, moving from state to state and exploring every patch of beauty along the way.

All of my kids are special, and all are very different. I stand in amazement when I ponder my three biological children, how they could have emerged from the same womb and all be so completely different from one another. My firstborn, Isaiah, was never once sent to the principal's office during all his years in school. He was never in a fight. . .he never talked back to a teacher. . .he obeyed all the rules, and would get so frustrated with me when I would break all the rules. My lastborn, Zachariah, gets a note sent home from school every day. His talking back has been elevated to an art form. He doesn't own a pair of jeans for twenty-four hours before the knees are ripped. As Isaiah taught me about God's quiet and gentle love, Zachariah has taught me that God has a wicked sense of humor!

Lonika is my oldest daughter, and although I did not give birth to her or raise her (she was adopted as an adult), she is the daughter of my heart. A single mother, Lonika works hard every day to provide for her daughter, Jayla. Lonni has a great sense of humor, and when she sets her mind to accomplish something, she does not give up. She is determined, focused and very gracious.

Shaylah has a tender, sweet heart. Like my firstborn, my secondborn was also graced with a very gentle spirit. She is not a rough-and-tumble sort of girl the way I was. She moves with grace and is always a peacemaker, not a troublemaker like her momma!

Emanuel, Tanginique and Trey Jerome are siblings—all born to the same mother but with different fathers—whom I adopted out of our very broken foster care system. Tragically, they were even more abused by foster care givers than they were by their drug-addicted mother. Because of all the upheaval and abuse in their lives before they came, in their early teens, under my care, Manny, Tangi and Trey Jerome have attachment issues, and they all left my home less than five years after I adopted them. All three have beautiful smiles, outgoing personalities and strong wills to survive. The youngest of the three, TJ, works for me now and lives close by with his girlfriend and his infant son. When TJ found out Abbi was pregnant, he was only eighteen. I'm so proud of the way he stepped up to the plate and vowed he would be the father to his son that he never had, and of the way he parents his son. He is totally committed to his baby and to his fiancée and works hard every day to provide for his young family. When I see TJ holding Nehemiah, and talking to him with such deep love, I know the many trials and tribulations that I went through when Trey was a teenager have paid off. We are far closer today than when he came into my life at the age of nine, and I pray that one day his siblings will also decide to walk away from the trauma and poverty of their current life and walk back into the family that is waiting to welcome them.

My two youngest boys are Zacky and TK (Thomas Karlton). TK also became a part of my life through adoption. A woman who facilitates adoptions contacted me one day, wondering if I knew anyone who'd be interested in adopting a young African-American toddler whose fourteen-year-old mom felt overwhelmed. I asked her to send me photos and information, and I'd make inquiries. Less than a month later, two-year-old Thomas Karlton was a part of our family. It was an impulsive decision on my part, and the timing wasn't the best, as I was going through a divorce and Zacky had been diagnosed with mild autism and other special needs. But something about TK's wide dark eyes melted my heart, and I couldn't bear the thought that he might have to go into foster care. TK is always eager to help and please others. He has a huge bright smile, and loves to play silly games, like crawling on his knees on the floor and pretending to be an alligator or a space monster, as he chases his younger sister and nephew.

And as I write this, I have just adopted two more children, daughters from Ghana, Africa, whom I've come to know on my mission trips there. At thirteen, Angel is a tiny slip of a girl, just six months younger than my mini-me, Shaylah, but she is over a foot shorter and weighs just seventy-five pounds. She has suffered malnutrition all her life, as well as malaria and other diseases. Blessing is only four. The day the adoption was final, I took the girls out to breakfast to celebrate. Angel and even little Blessing ate six eggs apiece! They had never seen a smorgasbord before, and could not stop returning for more boiled eggs.

It seems most of my adult life has been spent folding

laundry and trying to come up with creative Halloween costumes made from paper bags and pipe cleaners, screeching "Get in your car seat!" and "Stop hitting your brother!" and driving carloads of kids on field trips. But each day my children teach me. About patience. About forgiveness. About life. About love.

What have you learned from your children? And equally important, what are they learning from you?

> "A friend is someone who knows the song
> in your heart and can sing it back to you
> when you have forgotten the words."
>
> —Unknown

After the family, the next stage in our education about love comes from friendship. Most of us can remember how proud we were as youngsters to have a "best friend." As adults, too, we cherish our friends—those special people in our lives who are there for us at the best and worst of times, who add the icing to the cake of our successes and bring light to the darkness of our sorrows. Rock music has paid tribute to friendship in songs like Michael W. Smith's "Friends Are Friends Forever," Bill Withers's "Lean on Me" and the theme song from the movie *Toy Story*, "You've Got a Friend in Me," by Randy Newman.

The joy of friendship has been abundantly mine. I have

been blessed to know some pretty amazing people thus far in my life, and for whatever reason, God has allowed me to peer inside the soul of some of His finest handiwork. Friendship is precious to me, and I am deeply thankful for my many wonderful experiences of this kind of love. My childhood friends Natasha, Dee Dee and Billy are still a big part of my life today. Dee Dee and I share so many memories of past stages in our lives, and often reminisce and laugh about our days in disco dresses and halter tops, and the guys we were trying to attract (and sometimes did, with mixed results) by wearing them. Janey, my producer, is a friend who is closer than a sister. We were roommates for many years, she was my birthing coach for my last two biological children and we've worked together for the past eighteen years. I know if I needed a new lung, Janey would be the first to try and donate hers. And because of the strength of the love my girlfriends share with me, each week, on the air, I bond with my "Friday nite girls."

As you read about the friendships here, think about your own "friends of the heart," and the difference they've made and continue to make in your life. You may find yourself agreeing with Ralph Waldo Emerson, who said, "A friend may well be reckoned the masterpiece of nature."

"To Where You Are"

Dear Delilah,

I have been a professional Santa for over thirty years now. I could tell you many stories, but there's one I especially want to share.

A few years ago I was at one of the Ronald McDonald Houses for their family Christmas party the week before Christmas. After I visited with all the children there, a mother came up to me and quietly asked me if I had time to go and visit her daughter in the hospital. Ashley was six years old and too sick to leave the hospital to see Santa, but she wanted to tell him something special. I told the mother, "Let's go right now!"

As we approached Ashley's room, one of the nurses told me the little girl had advanced cancer, and that her doctors didn't expect her to make it to Christmas. This took my breath away, and I sent her mother in ahead of me. Then suddenly I burst through the door with my sleigh bells jingling, and in a big, booming voice, I said, "Ashley, I understand you want to talk to me!"

The child got up on her knees with tubes running in and out of her, and said, "Oh, yes, Santa!" She had lost all her hair, but she had the bluest eyes I've ever seen. I walked over and asked her if I could sit on her bed, then I pulled her over on my lap. We talked and sang

Christmas carols, and she played with my sleigh bells.
We visited and laughed for over an hour, until she fell
asleep in my arms. I tried to quietly lay her down, but
my bells rang, and her amazingly blue eyes popped open.

I said, "Oh, Ashley, I'm glad you woke up, I have
something very important to ask you. What do you want
for Christmas?"

She didn't have to think even a second. She said, "My
sisters want Teletubbies!"

Her one Christmas wish had come true—a personal visit from Santa.

I said, "I can do
that, but what do
you want?"

Again she didn't
have to think, and
said, "My brother
wants a Nintendo!"

And again I said,
"I can do that! But
what do *you* want?"

She thought for a couple minutes and then said
quietly, "I'm going to die soon, I know that, and I'm going
to go and live with Grandma and Grandpa and I'm not
going to hurt anymore. What I want is for Mom to stop
crying—she is going to be here alone and needs to take
care of my brother and sisters."

Speechless, I looked at this little angel. She could
have asked for anything from Santa, and all she cared

about was her family. I wrapped my arms around this beautiful little girl and planted a big kiss right on that cute little bald head. I told her, "Don't you worry, your mom is going to be just fine."

The mother had been doing some needlepoint, and I did something then that I had never done before and have never done since. I borrowed the mother's scissors, cut off one of my sleigh bells and gave it to Ashley. Then I wiped a tear from my eye, gave her mother a big parting hug, and asked her to keep me posted.

Christmas came and went, and I didn't hear anything. Then, two days after Christmas, I received the call that I really didn't want to get. Ashley had passed away that morning. I found out when and where the funeral was going to be. On the day, I dressed in my best suit and Santa tie and went to pay my respects. As I walked in, her mother saw me and came over. She told me that during Ashley's last week she had more energy and was happier than the entire six months since they found out she had cancer. Her one Christmas wish had come true—a personal visit from Santa.

It was an open-casket funeral, and I took a last look at Ashley. She was wearing a beautiful white dress, and they had put a long blond wig on her. She looked like the angel she was, and then, as I looked closer, I noticed that in her hand was my sleigh bell.

If you believe in angels, the most special angels are the Christmas angels, and I believe that Ashley is one of them. God bless you, Ashley, wherever you are, you've touched me in a way that no one else ever has.

In His Love,

Barry

"To Where You Are," performed by Josh Groban.
Songwriters: Richard Marx and Linda Thompson.

"MY FATHER'S EYES"

Dear Delilah,

Here's a story I'd like to share with you about a loving father—really *two* loving fathers.

During the Vietnam War, Uncle Sam called me to duty, and I was sent to a dangerous area, heavily infiltrated by the Vietcong. One eventful night, we were told to dig in. It seems that a couple battalions of VC were just over the hill. Well, there were only about 150 of us, including the clerks and cooks and the captain's hooch-maid. The VC could come right through us without so much as a second thought.

Let's keep praying for our children.

The night was long, but the next morning all was calm. It seems that Charlie just went around us! A short time later, I got a letter from my sister, one sentence of which I remember vividly to this day—"Dad prayed for you!"

Now I knew that my dad loved me and wanted me safe from all harm, but I never heard him pray in my whole life. I'm convinced he sensed my danger and said the prayer when he instinctively felt it was needed.

That was almost forty years ago, but it seems like only forty minutes. My dad has long gone to his eternal reward, no doubt thanking his Father in Heaven for answering his prayer. I pray for my son daily, as I'm sure most fathers do. Let's keep praying for our children. God is a great protector, and now you know why I said this is really a story about two loving fathers—mine and the Father of us all.

God Bless,

Al

"My Father's Eyes," performed by Eric Clapton.
Songwriter: Eric Clapton.

"BLUE EYES"

Hey, Delilah,

I've got a story about our family and the way God has loved and blessed us.

I have been married to my wife, Dawn, since May 29, 1993, and it's been a great journey so far. She always dreamed of having a little girl to dress up in pink and pass down her massive Barbie collection to, and began to dream of this daughter as soon as the first stick turned pink.

In April of 1995 we were blessed with a little boy whom we called Ben. Despite her Barbie dreams, my wife was as thrilled as I was with our healthy little boy—it was just the first baby, after all.

Well, Delilah, 2.5 years later we were pregnant again, and we were sure this time God was going to give us a little girl—one of each, right? Wrong! On February 14, 1998, we got our second son, Luke, who came at thirty-three weeks and spent three weeks in neonatal care.

Okay, now it's again 2.5 years later—September 2000—and after much fear we made it through the full nine months. . .and, yes, another son, Owen, was born. Of course we feel so happy having three healthy, blond-haired, blue-eyed boys, but there was just a brief "Not again" moment. Now we have two male dogs and a house full of males. Dawn has been a good sport about this and loves us to bits, as we do her. I used to make jokes, telling her I just never found the instructions on how to make a girl.

We believe there is a reason for everything, and Dawn and I decided to stop at three boys. We felt blessed to have such really good kids. Every time we passed all those adorable little girl clothes in the stores she would smile wistfully, but she never complained. She has two older brothers and no sisters, so she felt perhaps it was her destiny to care for boys and never have a daughter.

> Every time we passed those adorable little girl clothes in the stores, Dawn smiled wistfully.

Well, five years passed, and one day my wife said, "You're forty and I'm thirty-four, and it looks like if I'm ever going to get a girl, the stork will have to drop one on my doorstep." A week later she got on an elevator at the clinic where she works and ran in to a lady she used to supervise in her previous position. When Dawn asked her former employee how she was doing, the lady said, "Not so good." She had found out over the weekend that her nineteen-year-old daughter was pregnant and unable to care for a baby. My wife responded sympathetically and then went on her way. But the next day this lady called Dawn at work and told her that the daughter was having a girl and was going to give the baby up for adoption. She knew we had only sons—and maybe that Dawn had hoped for a little girl—and wanted to know if we would be interested in adopting this baby. Dawn told her she'd have to talk to me before committing herself, and was smiling nervously when I picked her up that day. Well, I put her fears to rest by saying of course we would be interested. That was in October 2006.

We met the birth mother at a restaurant and sensed that something was bothering her. We tried to make her comfortable, and she told us the father of the baby was African American and asked if that made a difference to us. My wife and I in perfect unison said, "So what?" My wife has brown eyes, whereas the boys and I all have blue eyes, and when we got in the car after our visit my wife said, "Well, I know I will finally get my brown-eyed girl!"

We then began a close relationship with the birth mother and her mom. We had agreed to an open adoption, so they came to visit our home on several occasions. On March 17th we were called to the hospital, and Mallorie was born to us as our St. Patty's little girl. We brought her home on the nineteenth, and we are approaching her first birthday now. The thing that gets me laughing is that our beautiful little daughter has blue eyes after all! So Dawn got only half her wish—but hey, she's not complaining.

This little girl has truly blessed our family and is loved by all who meet her. Her brothers have adjusted just fine, and she is attached to them as well. In the evening, I often work out in my garage, and I always listen to your stories on the radio there, so I thought maybe you would read our story. If this experience has taught me anything, it's that we cannot control the plans God has made for us. Timing is all His, and He's full of surprises.

Please pick something to play that will tell my wife and kids I love them more than anything in this world, and no matter what, I will be here as long as the good Lord allows to make sure they know they are loved.

Thanks for listening.

Sincerely,

Rick

"Blue Eyes," performed by Elton John.
Songwriters: Elton John and Gary Osborne.

"ANGEL"

Hi, Delilah,

You know how you always say, "Who's on your heart tonight"? Well, someone special is on my heart tonight, and I want to share the story with you.

I was born August 22, 1975, and on February 11, 1979, my mother was pronounced dead, due to medical malpractice. My baby sister was only nine days old. Of course, my whole family was devastated, especially my father. Faced with the terrifying prospect of raising four young children—ages nine, three, two and a week and a half—alone, my father had made the decision to split us up. We were each going to be raised by one of his siblings.

Except for the baby, we kids knew about the plan and were brokenhearted that we couldn't all stay together. But just when we thought all hope was gone, God sent us an angel. The day after my fifth birthday, my father married my mom's younger sister, and God gave us the best mother we could ever have had, outside of the one who gave birth to us.

Now that we're all adults, we've learned that our parents didn't marry for love of each other but for the love of us kids. There was no greater joy for us than to be able to stay with the family we knew and loved, without worrying about evil stepmothers or families where we would never feel like we truly belonged. And not only did we get a great mother out of the deal but an awesome sister as well!

This year my parents will be celebrating their twenty-seventh wedding anniversary and are more in love than they probably ever imagined they could be. My mother was only twenty-four when she took on the responsibility of raising five young children, and she sacrificed a lot. My dad worked full-time and was a pastor at our church. My mom gave up her job to be a stay-at-home mom. Not that she stayed at

> Just when we thought all hope was gone, God sent us an angel.

home much—it was nonstop running between after-school activities, sports and Scouts with us five kids. I'm sure there were many days back then that Mom felt unappreciated, but that sure isn't the case now. There are no words for just how much we all love and appreciate her.

And she is so selfless, so giving, so empathetic. For example, this past Mother's Day we got together to celebrate her, and instead she showed up with permanent markers and Mylar balloons so we could write a message on the balloons to our late biological mother. Together we wrote the messages and released the balloons. It was a very special moment—a gift from a very special mom.

Delilah, I just wanted to take the time to share my story of the love that I have for the woman I call Mom, whose love and support are constantly with me as I raise my own daughters.

All best,

Tracie

"Angel," performed by Sarah McLachlan.
Songwriter: Sarah McLachlan.

"I'll Be Home for Christmas"

Greetings from the Mideast, Delilah—

I've never written to you before, but I've listened to your show quite a bit back home. Currently I am stationed in Iraq and visit your Web site. I saw your appeal for holiday stories, and immediately began to reminisce about holidays past and what they meant to me. I share this not for recognition, but to reflect, as I write, about those times with family and friends that I hold dear to my heart.

We always had our Thanksgiving and Christmas gatherings at my grandparents' home back in Louisiana. And what a gathering it was! Every family member would arrive with a traditional holiday dish and/or gift, and it was always interesting to see what new friend they brought with them to share our celebration.

My brothers and I would immediately head to the backyard to play football while the older folks sipped coffee or eggnog or stayed busy in the kitchen preparing a feast. Even outside, we boys could smell the wonderful bouquet of roasted turkey, cornbread dressing, sweet potato casserole and, of course, Grandma's homemade pies. Apple, pecan, pumpkin, cherry, chocolate and lemon...I think everyone had a different favorite, and she never left one out. My favorite was the apple pie.

Grandma always relished watching everyone enjoy her pies. But mostly she took joy in seeing the whole family assembled under one roof, at one table. Holidays were the only time that busy schedules could be put aside and gathering as a family made the priority, as Grandma thought it should be.

Unfortunately, over the past few years, our grandparents and parents have all passed away, and with them the family gatherings. My brothers have married and scattered, and I, too, moved away and am now engaged. I miss my family terribly, and those few precious times we spent with each other every year.

> I can still smell Grandma's pies baking in the oven.

I've been fortunate, however, to find a soul mate whose family is much like mine was, a family that has adopted me as one of their own. They have those gatherings during the holidays and treasure them, just as my family used to treasure ours. The dishes may be different and the family memories ones I don't share; nevertheless, every year as I gather with my new family, I can still smell Grandma's pies baking in the oven. And then I know that all is well and that the family endures.

Thank you, Delilah, for allowing me to share my holiday story. I'm starting my third (and thankfully last) year here in Iraq, and I needed something to bring a smile to my face. I'm looking forward to three weeks' leave in December, so I can share Christmas and my twenty-seventh birthday with my fiancée and other loved ones. And also to remember those before them, who taught me so much about what the holidays mean and how truly special they can be.

Take care and may God bless!

David

"I'll Be Home for Christmas," performed by Michael Bublé.
Songwriters: Kim Gannon, Walter Kent, Buck Ram.

"LIGHT A SINGLE CANDLE"

Dear Delilah,

Children learn what love is from their families, and I'd like to share with you and your listeners the lessons I learned from mine.

As a small child in the 1950s, I stayed for a while with my great uncle and great aunt. Uncle Avery and Aunt Lucy loved children but never had any of their own, and they made it their personal mission to make sure that all the children in our extended family received at least one gift.

> I learned about sharing, compassion, duty and how even a small child can help.

These surrogate parents also taught me the true meaning of Christmas. A few days before Christmas, Uncle Avery would bring in bags of fruit, nuts and candy. Aunt Lucy and I would collect paper bags and boxes, colorful ribbon and other trimmings. They showed me how to fill the bags, and then Uncle Avery or Aunt Lucy would say, "This family is having a bad year, Brenda, put a little extra in those bags."

On Christmas Eve, we drove around four counties, leaving boxes and bags for the children, and sometimes money or bolts of cloth. I learned about sharing, compassion, duty and how even a small child can help do God's work on His Son's day.

Delilah, in memory of my "parents," thank you for your wonderful program, and please play a song in memory of Uncle Avery and Aunt Lucy. Thank you, Delilah.

God bless,
Brenda

"Light a Single Candle," performed by Anne Cochran. Songwriters: Jim Brickman, Delilah Rene.

"THE ROSE"

Dear Delilah,

I have an amazing story about my grandmother, Ruby, who died of colon cancer when I was four years old. Whenever I look at a rose, particularly a yellow one, I think of her. Here's why. . . .

A few years before she left us, Grandma went with my grandpa to a local nursery to pick out rose bushes. Grandpa picked out two bushes. Grandma picked one—yellow roses, which were her favorites. When they got home, they planted the three rose bushes in a row, with Grandma's in the middle. As time went by, not one of the rose bushes bloomed. Grandma got very sick with cancer, and there were still no roses.

> Whenever I look at a yellow rose, I think of Grandma Ruby.

Then, on the day Grandma passed away, Grandpa was in the garden when he noticed something unusual. Grandma's bush had a single bloom on it. Grandpa took a picture of that yellow rose, because there was never a bloom or bud on that bush before (and there hasn't been since).

My mom considers that beautiful yellow rose a goodbye kiss from Grandma. I'm thirteen years old now, and I still feel Grandma Ruby by my side every day, wherever I go. My mom says she feels Grandma's presence as well. In her final hours, Grandma Ruby fought to keep living until all of her children were there in her room. As soon as my aunt closed the door, Grandma stopped breathing. Our whole family loved my grandma Ruby, and I will never forget her.

Love,

Audrey

"The Rose," performed by Bette Midler.
Songwriter: Amanda McBroom.

"Give It Away"

Dear Delilah,

We would like to start by thanking you for providing such a wonderful program to listen to. In this world of violence, sensationalism, scandal and negativity, a program that is encouraging, uplifting and inspirational is a welcome oasis.

Our story is about a love of family—all of God's family. Seven years ago, a group of us were riding together in a van in Mexico. The topic of conversation was "What would you do if you won the lottery?"

The usual answers were given—"buy a big house, take a cruise around the world, retire," etc. But when the question came around to my wife, Kim, she replied that she had always wanted to do something for the world's poor, like providing food or safe drinking water. A gentleman in the van replied that Kim didn't need to win the lottery to do those things, and it just so happened that he was on the board of directors of an organization that provides safe drinking water to communities and villages in underprivileged countries.

After returning to our busy and (all thanks to God) successful careers, Kim and I felt the call to give back some of what we have been blessed with. Five months later we found ourselves on our way to Ecuador to fund the installation of a safe drinking-water system in a rural village. We visited two communities to which water systems had already been donated and two candidate villages, of which we were to choose one to receive a water system. Our experience was so moving that we decided to fund both systems. For the cost of a private well for a single-family home here in the States, we were able to provide safe water for a village of five hundred people.

This experience was so gratifying, we realized that we had found a new purpose in life. Upon returning home we recruited friends and family to join us in our newfound mission. We also started partnering with other organizations in Nicaragua and Guatemala, leading teams of volunteers on short-term mission trips multiple times per year. We've been involved with disaster relief efforts, installation of numerous water systems and latrines, the building of homes and schools, numerous medical clinics and clothing distributions. The best part, however, wasn't the fact we were able to provide for these physical needs—it was our ability to work as servants of God to provide hope, faith and love by answering the prayers of those in need. To let them know that they are truly loved and not forgotten.

In August of 2005 we were informed of severe child malnutrition and starvation due to drought, famine and poverty in southeastern Guatemala. The horrible plight in this area is virtually unrecognized by the rest of the world. In some villages the child mortality rate is as high as 33 percent. We decided to shift our focus to this part of Guatemala. We created our own nonprofit organization, called Outreach for World Hope. Our goal is to help save the lives of thousands of starving children and their families. We have created a "Virtual Village" child sponsorship program that identifies children most at risk. Even before a child sponsor is found, these "code red" children are enrolled in our program, provided with thirty days of in-patient nutritional rehabilitation, a monthly supply of food for their families, medical treatment, social services and—most important—hope, faith and love. We also offer the sponsors the ability to join us on a short-term trip where they can meet their sponsored child and the child's family.

> Kim and I felt the call to give back.

As you can imagine, this task is overwhelming, and we need all the help and sponsors we can get. So, we would like to make two requests: (1) Please check out and pass on the address of our Web site— www.outreachforworldhope.org. Be sure to look at the before/after page to see the difference people are making. And (2) I'd appreciate it if you could play a song as a thanks to the hundreds of people who have helped us so far, to those that are inspired to help, to my awesome wife who has dedicated her life to this work, and most important to God, who has taught me that it is definitely "better to give than receive."

Thank you, Delilah, for taking the time to read this. I pray for all of God's blessings on you and on your ministry.

With all of God's love,
Randy (and Kim)

"Give It Away," performed by Michael W. Smith.
Songwriters: Amy Grant, Wayne Kirkpatrick and Michael W. Smith.

"GOD BLESS THE CHILD"

Hi, Delilah,

Things happen for a reason, but we don't always realize it at the time. I'm thinking of how our own experiences growing up prepare us for being parents, and one childhood experience of my own in particular.

In my class in junior high there was a special needs student who longed to be one of the "cool" kids. The popular crowd knew of this boy's desire, and one day I heard them saying, "Let's mess with the retard." That cruel term was used by all the kids back then, including, I'm ashamed to say, me. Anyway, next thing I saw was a group of these kids going over to the boy and acting like they were his friends, and then one of the prettiest girls told him she wanted to be his girlfriend. The boy had no idea they were mocking him, and his whole face lit up with joy.

This incident made quite an impression on me. I found myself imagining the special needs kid going home all thrilled and telling his parents that he had "cool" friends and a pretty girlfriend. His parents would guess the truth but feel they had to pretend to believe the story lest they break his heart by letting him know the other kids were making fun of him. Of course, the kid's illusions didn't last long, because the next day in school, his new "friends" wanted nothing to do with him. I imagined him going home in tears this time and his parents being even more brokenhearted now that their worst fears had been realized. I felt sick. From then on, I believe I became a kinder person, more sensitive to other people's feelings, especially if they were in some way "different."

Now I'm thirty-five, married, and have four beautiful kids of my own. My life is their life. Everything I do is for them. But our twelve-year-old has Asperger's syndrome, a form of autism. Though he has the biggest, kindest heart in the world and is extremely intelligent, he has

Our son will always find love at home.

the social skills of a five-year-old. Now my wife and I are the parents whose child sometimes comes home from school crying because other kids are picking on him, or making fun of him because he is different. He has no idea why they do this, and asks us, "What did I do to them?" or "Why are they so mean?" My wife and I do our best to comfort him and let him know he will always find love at home.

I'm glad I witnessed those kids being mean back when I was in school; it raised my consciousness and made me better-equipped to be the parent of a child with Asperger's. I'm sure there are other parents like us, struggling with their children's pain, and I hope you can find a song that will encourage people to be kinder, for the sake of both the kids and their parents.

Thank you,

Max

"God Bless the Child," performed by Shania Twain.
Songwriters: Robert John "Mutt" Lange and Shania Twain.

"Grandma's Hands"

Dear Delilah,

This morning, Friday, March 16, 2007, at 5:30 a.m., my grandma passed away. She was such a kindhearted, caring lady—her motto was "Share with God's people who are in need" (Romans 12:13)—that I want to tell you and your listeners about her.

When my brother and I were little, Grandma often took care of us. She'd come over early in the morning—my dad worked the night shift, and Mom would leave for work when my grandma arrived. I still remember how much fun it was making clay cookies with her. Grandma would roll out the soft and pliable clay while my brother and I removed the boxes of cookie cutters from the cabinet. Grandma had her cookie cutters divided into individual boxes, with the metal, plastic, ceramic, animal-shaped, holiday cutters, and many more, all separated. Grandma invited my brother and me to each take the cookie cutter of our choice. My favorite one was a six-sided metal cube with a different animal on each side. But Grandma's favorite cookie cutter was a red, heart-shaped one that printed the words "I Love You" on a heart-shaped cookie. This cookie cutter's handle was taped together. It was cracked on the top but still always created a perfect clay cookie that was made with love. Since Grandma had so many cookie cutters, I gave her the nickname "Grandma Cookie Cutter."

Grandma Cookie Cutter didn't just make clay cookies, of course. One of her specialties was her sugar cookies. She made them for every holiday. However, her major cookie holiday was Christmas. These cookies were rolled out then cut into shapes that included two different angels, two Santa Clauses, three different-sized trees, a snowman and a star. Grandma would bake the cookies until they were golden brown, then top them with homemade colored frosting. I always went over to help Grandma Cookie Cutter decorate these tasty, delicious cookies, and help her fill many containers with cookies to give to family and friends.

Grandma Cookie Cutter created wonderful memories for everyone who knew her.

Everyone who received a container of cookies would say they were the best sugar cookies ever. When Grandma baked her cookies at Christmas time, she also sent sixty-two containers to the people in Hospice, The Learning Centre and various nursing homes in the area. Grandma's generosity made other people's lives a little brighter around the busy holiday.

Donating cookies was just one of my grandma's good works. As part of World Relief, she and the members of her church collected donations of soap, clothing and school supplies. Grandma boxed up the soap and clothing like she did her Christmas books. The soap and clothing were sent all over the world to people who needed them. My grandma also made school kits out of supplies that were donated to her by members of the church. These kits included pencils, markers, crayons, notebooks, paper, erasers and plastic scissors. Grandma put the contents into a little white canvas bag and sent these kits all around the world. One time Grandma received a letter from a little girl in China who had the privilege to get a school kit. Grandma valued education, and would do anything to help children get a good one. I can still remember how she would read stories to my brother and me as we snuggled up against her on the big brown, comfy couch.

As you can see, Delilah, my Grandma Cookie Cutter was a thoughtful, talented and loving woman who created many wonderful memories for me and for everyone who knew her. She was one of the most important, as well as most interesting, people in my life.

My Grandma Cookie Cutter will be greatly missed. Could you please play a song in her memory? Listening to you over the past couple of weeks has kept my spirit up.

Thanks,

Laura

"Grandma's Hands," performed by Will Downing. Songwriter: Bill Withers.

"You Raise Me Up"

Dear Delilah,

I love the sharing of stories on your show and would like to share one about my family.

My mother had six children and sixteen grandchildren. We were the proverbial big, happy family until about a year and a half ago, when my two-year-old nephew fell into my mother's decorative pond and drowned. This was the worst loss we ever had to face.

My family all live in Missouri except me. I live in Iowa, and they called at two in the morning to tell me about the accident. At that point there was still hope, but the outlook was grim. I set off for the long, weary drive to my mother's house. On the way, I heard Josh Groban, singing "To Where You Are." I thought that this song, with its promise that our loved ones are in heaven, would be a comfort to my family. It was the first time I had ever heard Josh Groban's wonderful voice.

When I finally reached my mom's house, we received the call that my nephew was not going to make it. We all went to the hospital, where my sister had gone with her son in the ambulance. Her clothes were still wet from when she'd taken my nephew out of the pool, and her face was beet-red from crying so much. It took every bit of strength that I had to hold back my own tears.

Suddenly I felt an enormous anger at God. I wanted to scream at Him for taking one of our children.

Just then we got a call at the hospital that my brother's wife, who was almost eight months pregnant, had gone into labor. There were complications and she had to be airlifted to Des Moines. At the hospital there, she gave birth to a very small baby boy. As we were all assembled waiting for news, the doctor came in and said that the new baby was very sick and might not make it through the night.

My mom had faith that a hug and a kiss cures all.

Now more than ever, I was furious with God. How dare He take the most precious treasures in our lives!

There we were at the hospital where our baby was fighting for his life, when we suddenly heard Josh Groban singing "You Raise Me Up." My whole family had been sobbing uncontrollably and praying, and this amazing voice was like the voice of God responding to our prayer.

We weren't supposed to touch the baby, but my mom, having faith that a hug and a kiss cures all, picked him up and held him close.

The nurse came in and reminded my mother that

we were told not to pick the baby up because it could cause more complications.

My mother kindly said, "Sweetie, I believe that if God wants to take this child home with Him, He will do it whether we hold this baby or not. We would just like to let him feel the love while he is still here."

Then my mother prayed out loud:

"Dear Heavenly Father, Our life has been blessed with the greatest love, respect and joy. You have brought us through so many hard times and walked with us through so many great times. Father, I know that You have a plan, and no matter what, we will do Your will. This baby is a great asset to our family. We do not want to lose this precious life that You have brought to us. I ask, Father, that You give us a chance to teach him to be good, just as You have taught us to be. In Jesus' Holy and Precious Name. Amen."

A few hours later, through the tears and prayers, just as fast as tragedy had struck, so did joy. The doctor came into the room, performed some tests and said, "The baby is going to be fine and can go home tomorrow."

As we thanked God for the life He gave back to us, I begged for forgiveness for being so bitter.

Then I remembered Josh Groban. Just as God has lifted us up so that we can stand on mountains, that is what we would have to do for this family. . .and especially for my sister who lost her son and for the new baby.

I'm glad you play Josh Groban often on your show, Delilah.

Thank you and God bless,

Chrystal

"You Raise Me Up," performed by Josh Groban.
Songwriters: Brendan Graham and Rolf Lovland.

"He Ain't Heavy, He's My Brother"

Dear Delilah,

There are so many stories to come out of wars that people do not share. I want to share this one. It's a story about an enemy who performed the greatest act of friendship imaginable for me, thirty-four years ago on Christmas Day.

I was a soldier in the Vietnam War. On December 24, 1972, Christmas Eve, I was given orders to take my squad out and do a recon-and-ambush patrol, taking out any targets of opportunity. The squad was made up of eight men, including myself. About seven miles out of base camp we came across signs of enemy presence. We guessed their numbers were about the same as ours. But as we were setting up to ambush them, they ambushed us.

One by one my entire squad was killed before my eyes. I was the only one untouched. The enemy started to come in closer, knowing that only one of us was still left to fight. Surrounded, I continued to fire my weapon. Until it suddenly jammed. The next thing I knew was darkness.

When I came to, all I could see was bayoneted rifles. I heard someone scream something unintelligible, and saw the enemy back off. I lay there trying to wrap my mind around the fact that I was the sole survivor of my squad.

The NVR removed all my gear with great force, just

tearing away equipment. One punched me in the face. Then I heard the voice again, the one I'd heard screaming earlier, and everyone came to attention. It was the North Vietnamese lieutenant. He came over and gave orders to tie me up. I then realized how badly we'd been outnumbered—I counted thirty-five North Vietnamese soldiers in all. We moved out, leaving the bodies of my squad members behind.

It was hours until we took a break. The lieutenant said something in Vietnamese, and all but six men stayed. The rest went off into the jungle. We then left again, heading north. I was thinking how much I did not want to spend Christmas, let alone the remaining six months of my tour of duty, in a POW camp. We kept going north for several more hours, well into the night.

It was now Christmas Day. We finally stopped. I was bound to a tree with a guard posted to ensure I wouldn't escape. They were fixing a meal. The North Vietnamese lieutenant came over to the tree carrying two bowls, and ordered the guard to leave. He made a gesture indicating one bowl was for me. "Merry Christmas," he said in excellent English, and untied my hands so I could eat. The bowl contained rice with some meat in it, and my captor gave me water to drink as well. Then he started to talk to me. He said that he understood the importance of this day in American culture, and it would be an honor for him to celebrate Christmas with me. He told me his name was Nugent, and he had no family—the French had killed them all earlier in the war. Nugent had been educated in Canada, but when he returned to North Vietnam, he was drafted into the army. I was reluctant even to talk with him, afraid he would try to get intel from me about troops and units' strengths. But he continued to speak only of nonmilitary things. Here was my enemy, talking as if we'd been friends for years. I had been holding back, but now I entered the conversation as well—he seemed to have no interest in interrogating me, and it wasn't as if I had anything better to do with the time.

Eventually he suggested we could sing Christmas carols, but not too loud, so we wouldn't wake his men. He said his favorite carol was "Silent Night," and started to sing it. I was impressed with Nugent's voice, which was similar to Aaron Neville's—if he'd been a civilian, he could have been a professional singer. His voice was that great. I felt a calm come over me. I started to sing with him.

But I was no Nugent—my singing was more like croaking. When we finished the song, he told me, laughing, that I was a terrible singer. I wasn't offended—I knew it was true.

Nevertheless, we sang a few more carols together and then called it a night. The guard came back over, and Nugent retied my hands.

At daylight we started to move again, but now in a southwesterly direction. We walked for hours, until we came onto an open field. Then we stopped and the North Vietnamese looked around, scouting for danger. As we moved across the field, a shot rang out and one man went down. The rest hit the ground and returned fire. Bullets were flying all around.

Several of the men were killed in the first couple minutes of the firefight. My American comrades were winning this go-round. There were only two NVR's left, Nugent and the guard who had been watching me. The guard turned and raised his rifle to kill me. Nugent jumped up and got in front of me just as the guard pulled the trigger. Nugent took several rounds in the chest, and my rescuers shot the guard.

I crawled over to Nugent and held him in my arms. He spoke, thanking me for the Christmas songfest. I started to sing "Silent Night" to him, knowing it was his favorite carol and not knowing what else I could do for this man who'd done the unthinkable for me.

And then the strangest thing happened. What I heard come out of my mouth was not my own voice, but one of remarkable beauty. The sound was so exquisite that as Nugent put his bloody hand to my lips, he said, "Voice of angel, I go in peace. Thank you." At that moment I did not see an enemy, but a friend and a brother.

Nugent was still in my arms when the marines came into my area. They'd gone out of their patrol to gather intel when they'd spotted my captors. When one of the marines grabbed Nugent to pull him off me, I pushed him away. I told them what Nugent had done, and I requested permission to bury him. That was the least I could do for him.

Here was a man who started as an enemy, showed compassion, became a friend, died as a brother. Was it my youth, the fact that I still had family while there was no one to mourn him, that made Nugent want to give his life for mine? Did he even think it through, or was it just some inexplicable protective impulse? I'll never know.

Here was my enemy, talking as if we'd been friends for years.

At the time, I didn't really understand—although I was grateful for his sacrifice, in my heart of hearts I thought he'd been a fool. But over the years, my thinking has changed. I understand that Nugent's sacrifice was like that of Jesus, dying on the cross for us so that we might live.

Delilah, please dedicate a song to my brother Nugent.
God bless,
Hipshot

"He Ain't Heavy, He's My Brother," performed by The Hollies.
Songwriters: Bob Russell and Bobby Scott.

"THE GIFT"

Dear Delilah,

I am a forty-nine-year-old mother and grandmother who started to listen to you May 4, 2000. I've been inspired by the stories you've shared from your own life and your listeners', and now I have a Christmas story to share with you.

On October 25, 1970, when I was a seventh grader, my father passed away. My mother went on furlough from Hill Air Force Base in Roy, Utah, to raise her eight children by herself. She sent us back to school after Halloween, and the vice principal called me into his office for a chat. Mr. Cook said he knew it must be a hard thing to lose a father, and that sometimes the best way to work through grief is to reach out to others. He invited me to join the "Sub for Santa" drive at school, which was collecting food, toys and other goods to give to those in need over the holidays.

> Sometimes the best way to work through grief is to reach out to others.

In mid-December I was asked to be part of the delivery team. Mr. Cook and six of us kids went to play Santa, making stops and unloading presents and food from the van. When about half of the goods had been delivered, we started dropping kids off at their houses when we made a delivery near where they lived. Finally, I was the only student in the van, and Mr. Cook asked if I would help him with the last few deliveries. But after he told me a stop at a nursing home was our last delivery, I was puzzled, because it seemed to me there was still a lot of stuff left in the back of the van.

We came to my house, and I wished Mr. Cook a Merry Christmas and ran inside. A few minutes later there was a knock, and it was Mr. Cook with food, toys and other presents from the van: I sat on the stairs and cried, because it was all going to my house. The whole school had been collecting for us! The first day after the New Year, I went to Mr. Cook's office with a thank-you card from my mother, but now I want you to dedicate a song to thank all the students—seventh, eighth and ninth graders—who attended Sunset Junior High during the winter of 1970, for showing my family the true meaning of Christmas. I will never forget that experience with Sub for Santa. I told it to my children as an illustration of the JOY story: Christmas is to remember First Jesus, Second Others, and Last Yourself.

Thanks for listening to me, Delilah.

All best,

Kay Lynn

"The Gift," performed by Jim Brickman.
Songwriter: Jim Brickman.

"That's What Friends Are For"

Dear Delilah,

You are always promoting friendship and community among women, like your Friday nite girls, so I want to share with you a story about a group of girls who met by planning our weddings together online. We got together (virtually) on a Web site called The Knot on our local Pittsburgh board. We supported and advised each other during our engagements and up through the weddings, and by that time we wanted to continue the support group even though we were all married.

The Knot became The Nest. Instead of planning weddings, we started buying houses, starting families and doing all the other things that happen after "the big day." But it became more than that. Most of us have never met in real life, but we've been through a lot together. A great number of joyful events: new homes, births, adoptions, promotions, anniversaries and birthdays. And lately, a lot of sorrowful occasions. This year we've

> Whatever one "Nestie" needs, another is there to provide.

lost three husbands to death (one from suicide and two from cancer) and a couple more to divorce; mourned several deceased family members; survived illness, bed rest and miscarriages; and coped with fertility issues. In good times and bad, we have supported each other unconditionally. Whatever one "Nestie" needs, another is there to provide by lending a hand or a shoulder.

This is an amazing group of women, and I am proud to belong to it. I have been married for four years, and I still log on daily. I want to thank these wonderful women for the love, support and encouragement they share, so if you could find us a theme song, that would be amazing.

Gratefully yours,

Proud Pittsburgh Nestie Kristine

"That's What Friends Are For," performed by Dionne Warwick. Songwriters: Burt Bacharach and Carole Bayer Sager.

"Lean On Me"

Hi, Delilah,

I'd like to share a story about my best friend, Lynne. Any woman would be blessed to have Lynne as a friend—let me tell you why.

Lynne and I met nineteen years ago at the hospital where her now deceased husband and my daughter were patients. My daughter had been severely injured in an auto accident and to this day she requires twenty-four-hour care. I am so thankful to God I still have her, and I have assumed a lot of her care myself. For the first five years after she came home from the hospital, I never took a vacation, and finally, good friend that she is, Lynne told me I needed a break and that she was going to plan a two-day trip for us. I was able to find a relative to take care of my daughter while we were away.

Lynne had planned two wonderful days, with shopping and other treats, but even better for me was the night before we left. Lynne insisted I stay at her home, brought out a bottle of good wine, and we sat around talking and laughing until two a.m., just like a couple of high school girls at a slumber party. She then fixed us a cup of tea, had me lie on her sofa in front of the fireplace and turned on some relaxing music until I fell asleep.

Delilah, this was by far the best night I'd spent since my daughter's accident, and I will never forget it. Whenever I get depressed or worn-out, I go back there in my mind. I am so grateful for that night and for the best friend who made it happen for me. Lynne is still always here for me and my daughter whenever I need her. I would like to let her know how much she means to me and to thank her again for being the person she is!

Could you please play a song with a theme about friendship? Thank you so much. I love your show and listen every night, you always seem to have just the right words I need to hear at the right time.

You are a blessing to so many.

God bless you!!!

Mary

"Lean On Me," performed by Bill Withers.
Songwriter: Bill Withers.

"FATHER FIGURE"

Dear Delilah,

Every night during the Christmas season I listen to your beautiful radio program. You are always telling your listeners to "Love someone tonight," and I want to share with you the story of a unique act of love. I also want to thank, through your radio program, Father John Heropoulos, the Greek Orthodox priest who saved my son Michael's life by donating a kidney to him. Thanks to this angel, my son Michael, now twenty-one, just celebrated his fifth Christmas free of dialysis. We owe everything to Father John, and I would like to tell you the full story.

Michael's health problems began when he was two, and by the time he was fifteen, both of his kidneys were failing. Although my wife, Maria, and I would gladly have donated a kidney, we were not a match, and neither were Michael's siblings. We were told it would be anywhere from one to five years before a kidney would likely become available for Michael, and that might be too late. Already Michael was undergoing dialysis three times a week. He was unable to go to school or hang out with friends. The treatment was very painful, and our son was also suffering depression and hopelessness. His siblings, Vasilios and Anna Maria, were grieving for their brother as well.

By October 2002 Maria and I were feeling quite desperate. All I could think to do was to appeal to the Archbishop of our Greek Orthodox Church, and see if he could help us find a donor.

His Eminence Archbishop Demetrios forwarded my e-mail to the Social Services Department of the National Philoptochos Society. "Philoptochos" means "Friend of the Poor" and is the philanthropic arm of the Archdiocese of the Greek Orthodox Church in the United States. They sent a letter to all the Greek Orthodox parishes, and Father John, knowing he shared my son's O negative blood type, contacted the Philoptochos and asked if he could be tested as a compatible donor. When it was determined that he was a match, he asked the doctors at the Hackensack University Hospital in New Jersey to respect his wish to remain anonymous until the operation was successfully completed.

> We owe everything to Father John.

So, we learned that a donor had been found, but we did not yet know who it was. The surgeries were scheduled for May 12, 2003. There were some anxious moments as unanticipated complications occurred with both surgeries, but by God's grace the transplant took place and the new kidney began to function successfully in my sixteen-year-old son's body.

Three days later, we learned Father John's identity when he came into my son's room to meet us for the first time. He told us he had received several signs that he was meant to be my son's donor. "By giving Michael my kidney," he explained, "I was also thanking God for all the gifts I've been given in my life."

When he was sufficiently recovered, Michael wrote to the National Philoptochos office. In his letter, he said, "I don't think there is a word in the dictionary to express my thanks and gratitude to the beloved Rev. Fr. John Heropoulos for saving my life."

People like Father John should be remembered and honored during every holiday season. Delilah, can you please help us to commemorate this holy priest's gift to Michael and to our family by dedicating a song to him?

Thank you,

Demetrios

"Father Figure," performed by George Michael.
Songwriter: George Michael.

True Love

True love doesn't have a happy ending:
True love doesn't have an ending.

—Unknown

I love to get calls from listeners who have figured out the key to a long and happy marriage. You can hear it in their voices the minute they begin to speak of their partners. . .a sense of deep joy that is qualitatively unlike any other sound I have heard over the years. These people have known a powerful and abiding love that gets better with time. Unfortunately these calls are few and far between, and yet when I hear that note of happiness, I hang on to every word these callers are willing to share with me.

I probe deeper with these listeners—those who have been married fifteen years or more and still sound like teenagers falling in love for the first time, but with a wisdom and peace that comes with maturity. I have not experienced that kind of love in my own life, nor did I see it modeled in my family of origin. My folks stayed together for thirty years because of their kids, their community and their shared experiences. But not because they thrilled to know one another deeply or because they cherished their time on this earth together. Sad truth is, once my mom left the man she had complained about bitterly for most of her adult life, he died. And then she died shortly afterward. They couldn't live with one another, and yet it appears they couldn't live without one another, either.

I have met a few couples who met and fell in love with their life partner and shared their life as one. The church I used to attend teaches that this is the standard, the "norm" for people who love the Lord. But the truth is that loving God doesn't make you any more able to figure out how to have a loving, committed marriage than listening to love songs does. If it did, the divorce rate among the religious would be minimal, and statistics show otherwise. I remember reading about a huge study done a few years back in which less than seven percent of church members married ten years or longer told interviewers they were still satisfied with and joyful about their partner.

Even the Bible gives lie to the myth that those with faith will automatically find true love in marriage. Think of King David, so often cited by pastors and clergy and religious writers as an example of wisdom and faithfulness to God. He lived with passion and zeal. So much passion that he lost track of his wives and concubines. The Bible says King David was "a man after God's heart." But he couldn't stay faithful to one woman. He couldn't stay faithful to ten women!

Why did the man who loved God with all his heart not have a successful marriage? And why have so many wonderful pastors and preachers and teachers of the faith throughout the ages struggled with being happily married to one person? Why have they divorced? Or had affairs? Or just resigned themselves to empty marriages that bring them no joy? If loving God or reading the Bible could "fix" this, why do thousands of believers call my show every year to confess that they don't feel connected to their spouses? I don't know, but I do know that when people call in to my show who have figured out how to remain in love with their partner, it is a wonderful thing to hear. And when I see a couple walking down the street, her weathered hand wrapped gently in his gnarled paw, I get tears in my eyes. I wonder, how many births have they shared? How many family members have they buried and mourned together? How many nights have they fallen asleep in each others' arms? How many cups of coffee or tea have they prepared for their beloved as they greet a new morning?

These people know each other, and real love is simply knowing. It is knowing their hopes and their dreams, their special gifts and talents. It's also knowing their character defects and their deep, dark secrets. It's knowing that they look best in the morning light, with their hair slightly tussled and sleep in the corners of their eyes. It's knowing that they are afraid of spiders or death or open heights. It's knowing that their mother loved them best, or not at all, and that their father taught them to work with wood in the shop or how to build a car, or that he hit them on the back of the head for minor infractions of the family rules.

True love is knowing someone so well, so deeply, so completely, that you feel a connection to them that goes beyond anything that can be described with words. Sometimes music comes close, like classical pieces that seem to describe the essence of someone's soul, or haunting ethereal songs by Enya, or a driving beat by the Doobie Brothers (which always brings my deceased brother back to me).

Sexual intimacy is a part of that knowing. When you know someone's body, their passions and delights, you connect to their soul on a deeper level. When you have shared the depths of your bodies, you have become one physically with another. Which is one of the many reasons why divorce or broken bonds of love hurt with such intensity. Because becoming "un-one" is much harder than becoming one. And to know someone on that level, and then to know that someone else will be that connected and close to them is gut-wrenchingly painful.

True love, the kind that doesn't go away, is knowing what makes someone's heart soar, and what kind of coffee they order. It's knowing what song lyrics bring tears to their eyes, and what movies make them laugh out loud. It's seeing an old beat-up car on the road, and remembering the one you love drove such a car in high school. It's knowing someone so well that when you see their favorite color in a painting, you smile and think of them. It's hearing the lyrics to a song that you have heard before, and realizing it was written just for them.

Knowing someone is feeling their heart beat, even though they are miles, or even an eternity away. My mom has been gone for more than a decade now and still I feel her hands on my forehead when I have a fever, I feel her heart beat when I lay my head on my feather pillow and pray for my own children's well being.

"Death cannot stop true love, just delay it a bit," said fair Wesley to Buttercup in *The Princess Bride*. True love is knowing another, heart and soul, and death cannot diminish that knowledge. I have shared such sweet and deep love with a few who are far from lovers—my firstborn son and my girlfriends Janey and Gina; my daughter Shaylah and my late mother, Wilma; my youngest sons, Zack and Thomas; and even a prostitute named Angel who lived with me once.

These stories of people who found their true love, and made that love last against all odds, affirm that everlasting love does exist and, like the biblical pearl of great price, is the greatest treasure on earth.

"LOVE OF A LIFETIME"

Dear Delilah,

At the most terrible time in my life, the most wonderful thing happened to me—I fell in love! Here's my story. . . .

I was diagnosed with breast cancer at age thirty-four and had a single mastectomy. After eight months of chemo and radiation, I felt like I had been run over by a bus. Self-image? What self-image!

Then, one Sunday in December, I met Rob. From the first moment, for both of us, it was as if we had found our long-lost soul mates. We had so much in common, and the most important thing was that I liked *myself* when I was with him. We became inseparable. Everything in my life was now terrific—Rob was my #1 blessing, but I also felt fortunate to be back at work and surrounded by a supportive family.

Then, in February, I had a recurrence of cancer—only this time it came back in my bones. I spent some time in the hospital, and Rob never left my side. He wrapped his love around me completely, making me feel safe despite the terrifying diagnosis. My parents marveled at how selfless he was, and so did I. Come July 4th, he proposed to me at the top of the Stratosphere in Vegas while the fireworks were going off all around us. I hadn't seen this coming and was both stunned and overjoyed. We have had a beautiful year.

Delilah, just last week they found the cancer in my liver. I am now gearing up for my second round of chemo and a not-so-great prognosis. Poor Rob. He has waited thirty-five years for his true love, and it looks like he will have only limited time with me. I can't help but feel a little cheated also. Yet when I shared my feelings with Rob, his only comment was, "Lauri, I was convinced that this kind of love was never going to happen to me, and I am just so grateful that it did."

> God put Rob in my life when I needed him most, and I will love this man forever.

Rob tells me that he loves me with the strength of ten thousand angels. I thank God for him every day. He respects me, cherishes me, comforts me, cries with me. . .and hopefully I can reward all of that with at least a few more years here with him. My health permitting, we are planning to get married in March.

God put Rob in my life when I needed him most, and I will love this man forever—both in this world and the next. Could you please play a song for my wonderful man?

Delilah, you also make such a difference in my life

with your genuine heart. I always feel so good after listening to you. After everything I have gone through, I have learned that the most important thing in life is never to lose hope. Hope is why I now have the strength to put my feet on the ground every morning—because I just don't want to miss a single minute with Rob. And you know what? Life is really, really good, even with stage-four cancer. Love makes all the difference.

Thank you so much for touching my life.

Sincerely,

Lauri

"Love of a Lifetime," performed by Firehouse.
Songwriters: Bill Leverty and C.J. Snare.

"I Just Called To Say I Love You"

Dear Delilah,

I want to tell you a story about my first and only love. It's so amazing, you'd think it was from the movies.

I'm a college student studying accounting. About two years ago I was browsing on a message board for creative writing, and I happened to come upon a particular story. After reading it, I was quite impressed and left a message for the author. He responded, and whenever I wrote my own stories he would leave a nice comment or two. This went on for about a year, till we finally told each other our real names (we had been using aliases). His name is Anthony and mine is Amy.

We discovered many common interests. Anthony is also a college student—he's

I was the first to say "I love you," which was a huge thing for me.

planning to become a teacher. He and I both love to write fan fiction, original stories that feature our favorite characters from TV shows. Also, we both love music. We had a page on the board just devoted to music. We'd post lyrics to our favorite songs as our way of serenading one another. Our musical tastes are a bit different though—he likes classic R&B, gospel and oldies, while I like alternative and rock. Interesting combo, no?

To elaborate on how we became "official": I'd been hurt before and was very, very scared of letting Anthony know how I really felt, so first I tested the waters. I asked his advice on what I should do if I liked someone (he had no clue that it was about him), and he said, "Tell the truth." So on November 8, 2006, I told him that I was crazy about him but had been apprehensive about saying so because I'd been hurt so much before, and because his living in California while I'm in Arkansas would make things difficult.

I was the first to say "I love you," which was a huge thing for me. His response was all I could wish for. He said that he was aware of the distance thing but he wanted to make it work, and he said he loved me, too.

We soon began to e-mail one another, sending pictures with the e-mails. Anthony is a handsome Hispanic with black hair, brown eyes and the biggest smile. I'm a Caucasian with brown hair, glasses and blue-and-gold eyes. The more we began to communicate, the deeper our feelings became for one another.

We have pet names for each other. He's my "honey bunny" and I'm his "sweetcakes." I used to think those were cheesy. . .actually, I still do, but when I hear him call me sweetcakes in that special way I can't help but call him honey bunny. He always makes a point to tell me how beautiful he thinks I am and he's just so romantic. We celebrated our six-month anniversary in May and he got me a beautiful Brighton timepiece that I wear all the time.

We finally met in person at the end of May and into June of 2007, and it was the best time of my life. My family loves him. Then, in August, my mother and I made the trip to California to meet Anthony's family. Our mothers got along wonderfully—yet another good omen. From there on, it has been an amazing journey for us. Of finding out who we are and who we are to each other. My only complaint is about the distance. Everyone has told me that long-distance relationships don't work, but this is too special to let go, and neither one of us wants to.

As I mentioned, he's my first, and *I'm his first*. We'll have been together for a year this coming November. He hasn't asked me to marry him yet—we're going to wait till he's finished with college and I see what it's like to be on my own (I'll get my associate degree this year, but Anthony is going on for a bachelor's). I know he's the one God made specially for me.

I hope this has put a smile on your face and in your heart to see that true love does exist for everyone, even for those who never thought it was going to happen.

God bless,

Amy

"I Just Called To Say I Love You," performed by Stevie Wonder. Songwriter: Stevie Wonder.

"I FINALLY FOUND SOMEONE"

Dear Delilah,

My mother and I have listened to your program for years. After all your words of sympathy, guidance and support I wanted to share this story of hope with you. My story of finally finding love.

I met my now-fiancé at a bar a year ago. Perhaps not the most romantic of places, but this entire relationship has taught me that things happen when you least expect them to. Prior to meeting Kevin, I was in a string of bad relationships with men who took more than they gave. They were selfish, and I was merely someone who fed their egos. I wanted so badly to find someone who could love me as much as I loved him, but I truly thought I'd never meet my match. And New York City wasn't giving me much to work with.

Then, two days before Christmas Eve, my brother invited me to a basketball game at Madison Square Garden. I was reluctant at first, but my brother mentioned one of his friends was bringing a single buddy along. Now the last thing I wanted was to be set up, but when I talked to my mother about it, she explained that you never know who you'll meet or what they'll be to you. She insisted I go and, taking her advice, I decided to live for the moment and meet this "buddy." Sadly, as I'd feared, there was no chemistry. He was a very nice guy with a good sense of humor, but there was something missing. Feeling completely down and about out of hope, I decided to meet my friend for a drink after the game. And that's when it happened.

I first noticed Kevin's laugh and thought how friendly and warm it sounded. He was sitting with a friend directly in front of me, and when I got a better look, I was instantly hooked. We wound up talking the entire night. There was this instant connection that I'd never felt with anyone before. And to think I almost didn't give him my number! I remember thinking that my mother was right. You never know who you're going to meet or what they're going to mean to you. I met the love of my life that night!

Kevin and I began dating immediately. He actually left me a message later that night asking if I was ready to go out with him ASAP. He was traveling home to spend Christmas with his family, so I said I'd be ready when he returned to the city, anxiously hoping I'd get a phone call. . .and I did, five days later, right as his plane landed. We agreed to meet the next day, and I couldn't wait. Although I appeared calm and cool on the outside, inside my stomach was one big bundle of butterflies. I've never used the phrase "love at first sight," but whatever it was that sparked in me when we met again came very close. From that day on we were inseparable.

So often one person falls madly in love and it isn't reciprocated, but with Kevin and me it was gloriously mutual! He told me the first month we were together that he was going to marry me. He said he'd propose in six months, that he just knew. And the thing was that I knew, too. I knew he was supposed to be my husband someday. It surprised me how fast and how deeply I could love him.

> So often one person falls madly in love and it isn't reciprocated, but with us it was gloriously mutual!

And it also scared me. I had been hurt so many times and worried that what we had—what I was feeling—would suddenly disappear. But I knew I had to let go of the past if I wanted Kevin as my future. One of the many things he has taught me is to just let go and live for every moment. So I let go. And in return I got the greatest gift. I got Kevin.

For the first time I feel like an equal to my partner. We are a team. He respects me and loves me no matter what obstacles we have to face. More important, he is my friend and my greatest confidant. Although it was a little longer than six months, I'm now engaged and couldn't be any happier or more in love.

I hope my story brings some hope for anyone searching for love. It is out there. . .just not where you may expect to find it.

All my best,

Diana

"I Finally Found Someone," performed by Bryan Adams and Barbra Streisand. Songwriters: Bryan Adams, Marvin Hamlisch, Robert John "Mutt" Lange and Barbra Streisand.

"Friends & Lovers"

Dear Delilah,

Here's my love story.

I moved to New York from the Midwest just two days after graduating from college. I knew one person in the Big Apple—my roommate. She was a girl I had become friends with in college who had moved to Manhattan six months earlier.

I moved with no job, no friends other than her and no support system. My roommate helped put me in touch with a temp agency, and I immediately started working regularly. I also got a part-time job working in a clothing store in the evenings.

It was at my second temp assignment that I met Jason. I ran home that night and immediately started telling my roommate how I was working with this really cute guy. . .how nice he was, and how I got to work closely with him since he was training me on the computer system, and on and on and on. Well, luckily for me, that two-week temp assignment lasted six months.

Everyone in the office knew how much I liked Jason, but even though I dressed in inappropriately sexy outfits to get his attention, he seemed clueless and never asked me on a date. Eventually I stopped trying to attract him. Instead, we became good friends. We'd eat lunch together, go out in a group setting with our friends for drinks and dancing or hang out. I had resigned myself to the fact that we would only be friends—at least it was better than nothing.

But I wanted Jason to be happy, and I knew he wanted a girlfriend. I figured, "If I can't have him, then someone else might as well." So I set him up with a girl I had become friends with at my retail job. They went out a few times, but there was no spark. She knew how much I liked him, and I remember her telling me, "You're going to marry that guy." I told her she was crazy.

Well, the day finally came that my temp assignment ended and I had to leave that job. Jason and I stayed in touch in the first month or so, but then we both got busy in our jobs and the phone calls diminished. We would see each other on our way to work from time to time, and we'd always wave enthusiastically to one another, but that was the extent of the relationship.

Then, about seven months after I left the temp job, Jason called me. We had a great talk; it was as if we had never lost touch. He wanted to invite me to a holiday party that his parents were having the following weekend. I, of course, accepted.

I remember walking in the door of his parents' house and meeting his mother. It seemed to me she looked at me the way a mother looks at her son's girlfriend. I had the weirdest feeling about it, because after all, Jason and I were only friends. What had he told her about me to make her size me up that way?

I met his dad, his sister and her boyfriend, cousins, an aunt and family friends. I had a wonderful time. They were all such lovely people, and I was happy to finally have friends in the city. When the time came for Jason to walk me out, he hugged me. And he hugged me. And he hugged me. I said goodbye and walked away, thinking to myself that he'd held on a little too long. That was not a "friend hug." Was I reading too much into it, or was something happening here?

Was I reading something into it, or was something happening here?

Two days later I got my answer. We had a long conversation, and at the very end of the phone call, he asked me out. Not as a friend this time, but on a real date. I was thrilled. I had known him for over a year at this point. Finally!

We had our first date on January 9th. The following March we moved in together. We got engaged that Christmas Eve and married the following December.

Fast forward nine years and we're still happily married and have two wonderful children.

My friend was right. . .I did marry that guy! Please dedicate a song to our love, Delilah.

Sincerely,

Amanda

"Friends & Lovers," performed by Gloria Loring.
Songwriters: Paul Gordon and Jay Gruska.

"More Than Words"

Dear Delilah,

I would like to share my husband Dan's story, because he has always been there for me and I want him to know he is an amazing and inspiring person.

Dan and I met as freshmen in high school and soon began dating. Thanks to Dan, I have fond memories of those teenage years. Upon graduation, I chose to go to college and Dan chose to join the U.S. Marine Corps. We promised we would stay together, but we had no idea what was in store for us. I never knew how much I truly cared for Dan until the day he left for boot camp. When you are with someone practically every day, you can't imagine what your life will be like without that person in it.

Dan left for boot camp on the fateful day of September 11, 2001, but due to travel restrictions after the terrorist attacks, he was sent back home for a week. We spent every day together during that week, and I felt sick to my stomach because I did not want him to leave again. Dan asked me if I wanted him to stay, and I could not bear to tell him the truth. Instead, I told him he needed to make the decision on his own.

Dan decided to become a U.S. Marine. The only communication we had was via mail. He was allowed

to make one phone call on Thanksgiving, and he chose
to call me. I recall talking to him with the biggest smile
and the largest tears rolling down my face. Three long
months later, Dan and I were reunited at his boot-camp
graduation at Parris Island, South Carolina. I remember
our embrace and the connection we both felt toward
each other. Never once did he mention himself unless I
asked. He wanted to know that I was doing well.

Dan remained in the marines, traveling around the
nation and world. I continued studying at college. We
made every effort to see each other. I saved up money
from my part-time job to visit every few weeks, and
he jumped at the chance whenever he was allowed to
come home, despite a twelve-hour drive each way.

In 2004, Dan was deployed to Afghanistan. On
April 24, he lost his left leg below the knee due to
an IED attack on the vehicle he was driving. I was in
college at the time this happened. I had spoken to
Dan a few days earlier. I clearly recall sitting in class
and hearing my phone vibrate. I saw a strange number
and knew it was Dan. I ran outside the classroom to
answer and I became weak. The sound of his voice
brought butterflies to my stomach, and this was
another moment where I knew I truly loved Dan.
He said everything was fine and he would be home
before I knew it. Days later, I received the devastating
phone call. It was an early Sunday morning, and I knew

something was not right. I was terribly afraid Dan had died and was so relieved to learn he had survived. My next thoughts were, "How he is doing? Is he scared? What can I do to comfort him?" I was able to call the hospital in Germany to talk to Dan for a few minutes, and again his only concern was that I was all right.

A very long week later, I saw him in person for the first time in months. I drove four hours, from college in Pennsylvania to the National Naval Hospital in Bethesda, Maryland. Both of us found our eyes swelling, and we hugged for a long time. I spent the summer of 2004 with Dan as he underwent surgery and rehabilitation at Walter Reed Army Medical Center. The day he walked on his prosthetic leg without any assistance was amazing, and he was so proud!

In the fall I had to return to college while Dan finished his rehabilitation. Again, the separation was hard to endure, especially after the intensity of the summer. But I graduated from college and Dan completed rehabilitation around the same time, and now we could plan for our future. We were married July 22, 2006, and are very happily married as I write today.

Come New Year's Day 2008, Dan and I will have been a couple for ten years. Each day is a blessing as we enjoy life together. And Dan has given me yet another reason to be proud of him by joining Team Semper Fi, part of the Injured Marine Semper Fi Fund.

My husband is on a mission to show others that a disability is no obstacle to living life to the fullest. As a Semper Fi team member since March 2007, Dan has competed in a number of running, biking and swimming events, such as the Virginia Beach Rock 'N' Roll Half Marathon, the Nation's Triathlon, the Alcatraz Challenge, the Armed Forces Triathlon and other events. His confidence has skyrocketed, and I could not be more proud of him. Delilah, please play a song to let Dan know that he inspires me every day and that I love him more than I could ever say.

> I never knew how much I truly cared for Dan until the day he left for boot camp.

Sincerely,

Jessica

"More Than Words," performed by Extreme.
Songwriters: N. Bettencourt and G. Cherone.

"Grow Old With Me"

Delilah:

I'd like to share with you my story about how a pen-pal relationship turned into everlasting love.

Back in June 1965, while at navy boot camp in Great Lakes, Illinois, I met a guy from Indiana who asked me if I would like a pen pal. Seemed his mother had written him a letter encouraging him to write to people from his hometown and enclosed a pretty long list of names. He didn't have time to write to all of them, so he asked me if I could write to a young woman on the list.

I wrote her, never thinking anything would come of it except a possible pen pal. She wrote me back, and we continued corresponding off and on for the next few years. At one point we didn't write for at least six months, but then it started up again and continued.

Then, in the spring of 1967, I received orders to

go on active duty. I wrote my pen pal about it, and she seemed kind of excited by the news. The letters increased in frequency between us from this point on. After I got to San Diego for training, I started looking forward to getting her letters. She sent me some pictures of herself, and sometimes on the back of the envelope, she'd put a lipstick kiss and write SWAK on it.

I finished my schooling and received orders to a ship off the coast of Vietnam in November 1967. During my leave before going overseas, I was able to go to Indiana to meet my pen pal. When I saw her in person, things seemed to heat up between us. On my way to the ship, I picked up a bottle of Chanel No. 5 perfume and sent it to her from San Francisco.

During my tour of duty aboard ship, I got to see a lot of the world: Japan, Taiwan, Hong Kong, Australia, the Philippines. My pen pal and I continued writing each other, and sending gifts. The letters got progressively more romantic as time went on. I thought about the six or so months where we hadn't written and realized I never wanted to lose my pen pal for that long again. So I went to the Fleet Exchange in Yokosuka, Japan, and bought a set of wedding rings.

In December 1968 I was released from active duty. As a reservist, I was in a position to marry, and we set a date: April 1969. After corresponding for almost four years, we got married, and my pen pal became my wife.

We've now been married for thirty-eight years. Yes, we've had ups and downs in our life together, but we have five kids, and five grandkids, with another on the way. The Lord has blessed us with a pretty good life, and we're getting closer to our goal of retirement.

Not bad for what I kiddingly call "my mail-order bride." Hope you have a great song for us, Delilah.

Thanks,

Clinton

"Grow Old With Me," performed by Mary Chapin Carpenter. Songwriter: John Lennon.

"MY LOVE"

Dear Delilah,

My story is about a love that's endured more than four decades—and about how I almost blew it by being a typical teenage guy (that is, a jerk!).

I was fifteen when I met my wife, Susie, and she was fourteen. At the time she lived in another state, although her grandparents lived near me and she visited occasionally. But we wrote regularly, and by our sophomore year she was able to come down for school dances with a girlfriend. The girlfriend was dating my twin brother, so that worked out well until I got myself in a pickle.

The problem was, by junior year I had begun playing the field, and a dance was coming up to which I had invited a cheerleader I was dating—but my brother had invited Susie's girlfriend, and Susie was coming with her. Worse, my conniving twin had actually written to Susie as me, and invited her to the dance as my date. She thought the letter came from me and accepted. So now I had two dates for the same dance!

> All I could do was pray to God to give me a second chance with Susie.

The cheerleader learned of the situation and decided that she wanted to size up her competition, so she suggested I take Susie to the dance while she would come with one of my friends. There didn't seem to be any alternative solutions to the problem, so I agreed.

Before we went to the dance, I did tell Susie that I'd been dating another girl, who would be at the dance that night. As you can imagine, that went over big. Not. You can see where this freight train is headed, and it's not looking good for lover boy. Did I forget to mention that the girls were the same age and shared the same birth date?

Delilah, why is it girls—and women—always have a way of getting together in the ladies' room and comparing notes? Boy, was I busted big-time. I had been dumb enough to get exactly the same gifts for both girls, not only on their shared birthday but for Christmas and Valentine's Day, too, as they soon found out. Well, they cried on each other's shoulders for about an hour, then made a pact to stop seeing me.

Since the cheerleader was the girl on the scene, I mended my fences there first, and succeeded in getting her to go out with me again. But now I realized it was Susie I really wanted, and after a few months I made a trip to see her. I was devastated to learn that she had found someone else and had no intention of ever seeing me again. All I could do was pray to God to take pity on me and give me a second chance with Susie.

Someone up there must like me, Delilah, because early in my senior year I ran in to Susie's dad, who told me that (a) she had broken up with her boyfriend and (b) Susie's family was moving to our town, where she would be going to the same school as me. I contacted her as soon as they moved into town, and Susie agreed to meet me for a talk.

When we got together, right off I apologized for my stupidity and told her that I knew she was the one meant for me. To my relief and joy, she told me that *she* knew the day she met me that we were meant for each other! Three weeks later I asked her to marry me after graduation. She accepted, and became my bride at seventeen. This August 19th we will be celebrating our fortieth wedding anniversary.

Our song back then was "Cherish" by The Association. This song has always expressed our feelings toward each other and continues to be our song. And there's another song by The Association that applies to us today as well. Susie's become self-conscious about the wrinkles and added pounds that come with aging, and sometimes she'll question how I can still desire her. I see in her eyes the question the song asks, if I'll ever get tired of her, and of course my answer is the same as the song's title: "Never My Love."

Many thanks,

Matt

"My Love," performed by Lionel Richie.
Songwriter: Donald and Richard Addrisi.

"You Are So Beautiful"

Dear Delilah,

I just have to share my love story with you. It's about my bride (and she is indeed my bride, even though we have never been able to afford a real "honeymoon." She has made me feel like a new groom every day since I met her).

I met my future bride, Miriam—aka Fezzle—in Hawaii in November of 1964, while I was stationed at Schofield Barracks and she was attending Honolulu Business College. Despite the huge rollers in her hair, the bulky BC sweatshirt, cut-off blue jeans and flip-flops, I was as smitten as the prince when he first spotted Cinderella at the ball. Don't ask me how, but I just knew her beautiful blue eyes saw right through me to my very soul.

Miriam and I became inseparable. Eventually, she graduated, my tour ended, and we left Oahu in April of 1966. On October 21, 1966, we said our vows to each other in front of God and a judge in San Antonio, Texas. It was not anything fancy or expensive. Just five bucks for the license and about a buck and a half for some gas, but that didn't matter to us because our souls had wed back in November of '64. In November of 1978, at the Temple in Salt Lake City, we repeated our vows to each other before God, the Prophet Spencer W. Kimball and the two missionaries who had found us, for time and eternity.

So far, we are taking care of the time part, and are looking forward to the eternity part of our lives together. We've had two beautiful children, a son and a daughter.

On December 31, 2002, Miriam had a hemorrhagic stroke. On January 4, 2003, the fourth day of her coma, her doctor called me into his office and suggested that I should make arrangements. He told me that her basal ganglia were full of blood and her ventricles were filling, and that she had less than a one-in-five chance of seeing the sun come up the next morning. I admit that I wasn't the brightest Bunsen burner in science class, but though I knew that the heart had ventricles, I had no idea that the brain had ventricles also. The doctor and the ICU nurses all assured me that Fezzle was not in pain, and that she would just slip away. Up until then, my prayers had been more like demands that God give Miriam back to me, but now I just said, "Daddy [that's how I talk to our Heavenly Father], You know I want Fezzle back, but if it's Your will to take her—well, I'm not crazy about that idea, but I'll accept it. Just don't let her suffer, let her slip away like the doc said."

> She has made me feel like a new groom every day since I met her.

Two nights later, Fezzle woke up. She was totally paralyzed on her right side, and barely able to speak. A lot of people urged me to put her into a nursing home, but, Delilah, I couldn't do that. My bride had seen me through too many tough times, had encouraged and taught me to become a decent human being, and I wasn't about to desert her in her hour of need. So, on January 29, 2003, knowing that she might be nothing more than a vegetable for the rest of her life, I took my Fezzle home with me. In the years since, she's gotten her voice back, some use of her right leg, and her sense of humor is the way it was when I first met her over forty years ago. I have been her only caregiver, and until recently never spent more than an hour away from her.

Delilah, could you please play a song for my wonderful bride, because her sweet good-night kiss kept my dreams sunny and warm during the recent ice storm, and her partly crooked smile every morning keeps my heart beating during the icy days.

May the love of the Heavenly Father, and all the gifts of Heaven, be with you and all your listeners.

Sincerely yours,

Jerry

"You Are So Beautiful," performed by Joe Cocker.
Songwriters: Bruce Fisher and Billy Preston.

"God Must Have Spent
a Little More Time on You"

Dear Delilah,

My love story is pretty amazing. I want to tell it to show how the union of man and wife can be a gift from God.

I was an abandoned child at age four, placed in a Native-American reservation school. While most children boarded at the school and went home on weekends/holidays/summers, my two brothers and sister and I remained year-round, attended by the nuns and priests who ran the place. We were told that a foster home was being sought for us, but it didn't happen right away.

My future foster parents were close friends with a young man who was becoming a priest and attended his ordination. He had been the best man at their wedding several years earlier. This priest was instrumental in having us placed in their home the following year. They had three children of their own, and had recently made a pact with the Lord. If He didn't send them any more natural children for a while, then they would consider taking in a child who needed a home. They ended up taking three of us—my older sister, who was thirteen at the time, was somehow able to return to our natural mother and grew up away from us.

When my oldest brother finished college, he returned to the Native-American reservation and worked in one of the mission schools as a counselor. He and his wife had twin boys, whose babysitter was named Jeanie. When the twins were two, my brother and his wife decided to return back home, so I went to help them move. The day we were to leave, a beautiful young lady with hair down to the small of her back came to the door to tell them goodbye. I met her very briefly—her name was Susie and she was Jeanie's sister. Jeanie was moving with my brother and sister-in-law, and would live with them and finish high school in our hometown.

> My feelings for Susie had deepened, but I wasn't sure what to do about them.

Jeanie and I became good friends. Her sister went on to college but found herself pregnant at the end of her first semester. Lost and a bit afraid, Susie finally 'fessed up to her mom. Her mom felt it would be best if Susie went to live in another town, and she thought of my foster parents, knowing how loving and supportive they were. They of course agreed, and Susie came to my folks' house to live and have her baby. I no longer lived at home, but was at their house when she arrived. Susie now had a pixie haircut and was sticking-out-to-the-moon pregnant. I could not believe this was the same young lady I had met several years earlier. We became friends during her pregnancy, but no more than that. She made new friends in the area and had much support bringing this baby into being.

My feelings for Susie had deepened, but I wasn't sure what to do about them. When the baby was about three months old, I was on a trip to Corpus Christi, Texas. I happened to be at a cathedral and felt that God wanted me to ask if I should pursue this young lady. Not being too familiar yet with the Bible, I opened to the story of Susanna and the wicked judges. Just the fact that I'd opened at the name "Susanna" was confirmation enough for me to pursue a deeper relationship with Susie. But I thought I should be patient until the timing was right, which was about four months later. Unfortunately one of my best friends had already asked her out and she had accepted. They hit it off and became a couple.

I still felt the Lord had chosen Susie for me, so I patiently waited on Him to end the relationship so I could go forward. Wasn't happening anytime soon! Buddy and I went on a vacation together the weekend

after Susie's sister got married. I finally brought up
the topic of our mutual interest in Susie and asked his
intentions. He said he was going to introduce her to his
family the following weekend. I assumed that meant he
was pretty serious. I then went back to the Lord and
expressed my dismay. I got a message in my heart that
I should wait for two weeks after we got back from our
trip, and if Susie and Buddy were still dating then, I
would know to move on. Well, two days before the two
weeks were up, my buddy told me their relationship
was over, that Susie felt that she needed to move in
a different direction. There was my opening at last! I
asked her out, and she accepted. We had three dates
and were married five months later, by the priest who
started it all by arranging my foster placement.

Susie and I are about to celebrate our thirtieth
anniversary next weekend. We have five children and
now four grandchildren. I would like you to dedicate
a song to her from me, Delilah. And thank her for her
trust in God, because when I told her I thought He
directed me to her, she never questioned it.

Let me update you about my foster parents as
well. Mom and Dad went on to adopt two additional
children, and took in another foster child. After all of
that, they placed their trust in God once again and said
they would no longer hold Him to the original pact (not
sending any natural children for a while). Good jokester

that God is, He sent them a new baby exactly nine months later. Naturally, they had to call this one Isaac. He is the same age as my adopted son, Keith!

Thank you, Delilah,

Robert

"God Must Have Spent a Little More Time on You," performed by *NSYNC. Songwriters: Evan Rogers and Carl Sturken.

"I'LL STAND BY YOU"

Hi, Delilah,

I want to share a story with you about an angel named Paul whom I met twenty-seven years ago, at my Christmas office party, and who is now my husband of twenty-four years.

When we met, I was seventeen and working part time in a family business—Paul, who was twenty-seven, was one of the sons of the family. For me, it was love at first sight. He shook my hand at the Christmas party to introduce himself, and I nearly fainted. I was in a fog over him. I could tell he was interested and asked him if we could go out, but he reminded me of the age difference and suggested, "Let's wait until you graduate from high school." He did come to my graduation and gave me a love-knot necklace. We started dating when I was eighteen years old.

The following year, on Christmas Day, Paul gave me an engagement ring at the family tree-trimming. Both our moms had tears of joy in their eyes. We were married September 10, 1983. Our love has been tested, especially through Paul's health. When he was twenty, he had cancer, and as a result one arm had to be amputated. However, that didn't stop him from working in the family business, and neither did stomach cancer, which he got seven years ago. In 2001, he was given a terminal diagnosis, but he has fought the disease and so far survived, to the amazement of all his doctors. Although he's had myriad complications, not to mention radiation, chemotherapy and surgeries, Paul has never complained and never given up the fight. He's been an inspiration to me, his family and our friends.

But that's not all, Delilah. Despite his illness, Paul has supported me through two jobs and four degrees, and he supports me now as I receive my master's in public health in December 2007. He's proud of my degrees and says supporting me was the least he could do, as I stood by him and took care of him all hours of the night and day. He likes to tease me that I'm the best Christmas present God could ever have given him.

> Paul likes to tease me that I'm the best Christmas present God could ever have given him.

Paul's liver is failing now, and he's getting weaker. I don't know how much longer we'll have together, and God didn't bless us with children, but He blessed us with True Love, and I'm not complaining. Whatever the future, I will always have my angel Paul with me at Christmastime.

God bless you,

Denise

"I'll Stand By You," performed by The Pretenders.
Songwriters: Chrissie Hynde, Tom Kelly and Billy Steinberg.

"I Cross My Heart"

Dear Delilah,

Sometimes you just know.

A few years ago I was working in a restaurant and met a guy who was a friend of my brother's. We got to talking and discovered other connections—my uncle and his mother had grown up in the same tiny town in Ireland, and we'd crossed paths a couple of times before.

Sean was fun-loving, attentive and good to be with. We went on a few dates, and I was growing really interested. Then he asked me to a college roommate's wedding—I was nervous but thrilled, because it was very early in our relationship for him to be asking me to be his date for a wedding!

I bought a new dress and shoes, got my hair and nails done, chose a card and waited anxiously for the introduction to all of Sean's friends. As we walked into the hotel reception area, Sean spotted a few people he knew and introduced me, but we didn't linger. He picked up the seating card, and we headed in.

I have to admit, I was a little surprised at the table. There was only one couple who seemed about our age—the rest were older to varying degrees, and they were dressed rather casually for a wedding.

Sean seated me and went to the bar to get drinks for us. Trying to be friendly, I asked the couple next to me if they'd gone to the church, and they said no. Then I asked the woman sitting near me if she was friends with the bride or groom. Giving me an odd look, she said neither—which puzzled me a bit. Sean was still at the bar chatting with someone he knew, so I thought I'd try to chat up the others at our table. They also looked at me oddly when I said Sean went to school with the groom.

I was feeling a bit off-kilter but trying hard to hide it as Sean headed back, smiling. Then a nice, elderly woman leaned across the table and said to me, "Where do you think you are, dear?"

Sometimes the oddest things tell you who is the person you're meant to be with.

"What do you mean?" I asked her, surprised. "Why, we're all at a wedding reception, to be sure!"

Now the whole table was smiling as the woman informed me, "But it's not a real wedding reception, dear. This is a performance of *Patrick and Maria*—a version of the famous *Tony and Tina's Wedding* play!"

Barely able to believe it, I looked up at Sean, who

had arrived with our drinks and was unable to hold his laughter in.

"You bought theater tickets and told me it was a wedding?" I said. "But I got a card! I bought a dress! I had my hair done!" All the same, I began to laugh, too—I could see the humor of the situation and how strange my remarks to the table must have seemed. Perhaps some of them thought I was one of the actors, being all too convincing as a "wedding guest."

"And you look lovely," he said gallantly. "I'm sorry if I put you to any inconvenience, Allison. I only wanted to see how you'd take the surprises that spending time with me would bring. It was a test—and you passed!"

Not everyone at the table got the joke—some were amazed that I didn't storm out. But Sean's trick was playful, not hurtful, so why should I be offended? It was a real icebreaker, and got our whole table chortling and talking in a way that might not have happened otherwise. We had a grand evening together and enjoyed the show.

Sean said that he knew at that point he would stick with me—and after five years of marriage, I guess I'll stick with him as well!

Sometimes the oddest things tell you just who is the person you're meant to be with. For me—and for Sean—it was a wedding that wasn't, and laughter that couldn't be held back.

Our wedding dance was "I Cross My Heart" by George Strait, and I'd love to hear it tonight, or any song that you'd like to play for us instead.

Thank you,

Allison

"I Cross My Heart," performed by George Strait.
Songwriters: Steve Dorf and Eric Kaz.

Lost and Found Love

Every parting is a form of death,
as every reunion is a type of heaven.

—TRYON EDWARDS, AMERICAN THEOLOGIAN

Stories of people reuniting with their first loves after many years apart always bring me to tears. Granted, I cry easily—anything from a wedding to a Hallmark movie to a picture of a deceased family member to the tragic story of someone I've never even met will start me blubbering—but there is something incredibly moving about these reunion romances. Love that is rediscovered after years of separation seems to be all the sweeter, as if the time apart did not diminish its intensity or its purity. When an old flame is rekindled, for most people it seems to burn more brightly the second time around. Maybe there are deep regrets that they let their true love slip through their fingers. Or maybe there were circumstances that prevented them from fulfilling their hearts' desire in years gone by—parents who objected or an age difference that mattered—that with the passage of time does not matter anymore.

I get calls from people who met their old lover at class reunions, at family weddings and family funerals, at kids' baseball games and at the grocery store.

There's a special joy I hear when listeners call in to share that they have reconnected with a love from yesteryear. The giddy excitement of their teenage crush is heard buried in their voice, layered with years of disappointment and heartache, and then finished off with new hope. School reunion Web sites, military alumni Web sites and hometown news sites all help to bring people back to each others' lives. The Internet may have some pretty dark sides to it, but coupled with the strange and wonderful way that God works in our lives, it has been instrumental in helping people reconnect with their first love on thousands of occasions and has produced a lot of "lost and found love" stories for my radio show.

Perhaps what makes these stories so satisfying is that they tell us you *can* go home again, that "lost" doesn't have to mean "lost forever," that true love truly does stand the test of time (and the intervention of life). We need to hear these messages, and that's what makes songs like "After All," sung by Peter Cetera and Cher, and Dan Fogelberg's "Same Old Lang Syne" strike a chord in so many hearts.

When I worked at WVBF in Boston, I met a cop named Steve. He was tall, handsome and very, very sweet. He was working through the painful mess of a second divorce, and trying to figure out how to care for his two boys, just a year apart, born to two different women. He had met Linda, fallen deeply in love and married her. They had a son together, and then he did a foolish thing—he cheated. That foolish thing resulted in a pregnancy, and he had to tell his lovely wife that he had betrayed her. Their marriage ended, and he tried to make things work with the mother of his second son.

All in all, it was amazing how well these two women worked things out so the boys, Ryan and Shawn, could share in each others' lives. And Steve did his best to be a good father and a good husband the second time around. Small problem. He was still completely connected to Linda, his first wife. Since we don't live in a country where multiple wives are legal, Steve did his best with his circumstances. When we met, he was divorcing the second wife, and mentioned he might bring wife number one to a comedy club where I was performing.

When he showed up with her, I was blown away. He had not mentioned, in all of our long conversations, how much he still loved her. Not once. And yet when I saw them sitting at the table together in the crowded night club, it was obvious the love they felt for each other had not diminished over the years.

When Steve called me the next day to talk, I asked bluntly, "*Why* are you divorced from this woman?"

He launched into the explanation of his unfaithfulness, and how sorry he was, blah blah blah.

I said, "And why are you telling this to me instead of Linda?"

He said, "She doesn't want to hear it from me. I broke her heart, and it's too late."

I couldn't believe he was so clueless. "Steve," I told him, "the look of love she has for you is so obvious it is pathetic. Call her and tell her all the stuff you share with me when you call this radio station at night."

He did. A year later I got to read a poem I wrote for them at their wedding.

In Luke 15, Jesus tells three parables about the joy of regaining something lost—the Parable of the Lost Sheep, the Parable of the Lost Coin and the well-beloved Parable of the Lost Son. I've had some experience with prodigal children and know the happiness of a parent whose alienated child returns home, but I don't have a personal story of lost and found romantic love. (I've lost and found romantic love more times than I care to count, but not with the same person. All those guys in high school that I used to think were The One moved on, as I did). Still, I've had the experience of being reunited with my childhood friends Dee Dee and Billy, who are once again close friends and neighbors after many years when we didn't even live in the same state. Because of these renewed friendships, I can understand the unique nature of a love that has roots going back decades, with myriad shared experiences—daily routines, triumphs, crises, perhaps even life-changing events.

The people we knew in our childhood and teenage years share so many memories and a common frame of reference; the lovers who awakened us sexually for the first time share a special moment of discovery in a way no one else ever can; our first spouses also share something unique with us, as do those with whom we once created a child, even if we didn't raise that child together. A lost and found love enables the lovers to reconnect not only with the person they once loved, but also in a sense with their own younger, more innocent and perhaps happier selves, and with a time in their lives that may have been happier as well. Whether or not our own love histories include a tale of reconnecting with a long-lost love and finding that the love has remained constant though the lovers have changed, I think we can all relate to this group of stories, and to the messages of hope and redemption they offer.

"Once in a Lifetime"

Hi, Delilah,

I used to listen to you in Holland, Michigan, in 2001 after I lost my first husband. There can't be two of you! My second husband shared you with me tonight, and I was elated to know you are here in the Carolinas now just like me. You are so inspirational! And I have for you an amazing love story about my "reunion romance"—thirty-eight years after the original romance!

My story starts back in the spring of 1967, when I met a wonderful guy in high school. We dated and I became pregnant. Keith asked me to marry him, but my dad said no. Since I was just seventeen, I felt I had no choice but to accept my father's decision. Our beautiful baby daughter was born in January 1968. Keith moved to Florida, and I later married someone else. We had no further contact.

Our daughter was adopted by my first husband, who was the only dad she knew as she was growing up. But later in life she became curious about her "real" father, and spent her vacations in Florida trying to find Keith. In 1994 her uncle asked her what she would like for her birthday, and she told him she wanted to find her dad. So, her uncle hired a private detective, who found Keith, happily married and living in North Carolina. He had been waiting all his life for that phone call. He was overjoyed to finally connect with the daughter he always knew was "out there somewhere."

Ten years later Keith lost his wife to cancer. Then he invited our daughter and our granddaughter down for the Thanksgiving holiday. In response, I wrote a brief letter to Keith expressing my appreciation for the fantastic dad he had become to our daughter. Then Keith called me and asked if I could come at the same time. A sort of reunion—we would take our first and only picture of the four of us as a keepsake.

> I put my heart on a shelf when we parted, and finally feel like a whole person again.

I decided I could make the trip. I am still here, and in April of last year we were married while our daughter and granddaughter were visiting. Keith's son was our best man. We are so happy and in LOVE again—or shall I say still? As for me, I put my heart on a shelf when we parted, and finally feel like a whole person again. I am an artist starting over here, and Keith is a retired letter carrier.

All our best to you and we will be listening often,

Verlie, Keith's wife (finally!)

"Once in a Lifetime," performed by Michael Bolton.
Songwriters: Leslie Bricusse and Anthony Newley.

"CHILD OF MINE"

Dear Delilah,

I have a story about a lost-and-found love, which is also a story about a "found" family.

My story begins in 1971, when I was a ninth grader secretly in love with a girl named Lynetta. Because I had—and still have—a severe stuttering problem, I was afraid to reveal my feelings to her for fear of rejection, but I did make friends with her by stopping by her table in the school cafeteria at lunch and sharing some really bad jokes. Because of my stutter, it took a while to get the jokes out, and now when Lynetta tells people about our shared past, she likes to say that before she could figure out the meaning of my punch lines, I was gone.

I didn't see Lynetta for a whole decade, when we resumed our friendship after reencountering each other at our tenth high school reunion. I had been divorced

> No child should be saddled with the term "step"-anything. They're children, period, and children are born to be loved.

for three years, and Lynetta's marriage was ending. We became CB buddies, and despite my stutter, I would call Lynetta—or "Rainbow," her CB call name—and talk to her for hours.

That fall Lynetta got divorced, and in January 1986 we got married—we're still together after over twenty years. But there's more to my story, because Lynetta brought into our family two beautiful children. At the time of our wedding, Tyra was eight and Kenny five. I was somewhat scared about becoming a stepfather as I'd never even had any children of my own, so I asked my maternal granddad what he thought about my taking on stepchildren. I still remember his reply: "Bobby, there's no such thing as a 'stepchild,' and as far as I'm concerned Tyra and Kenny are my grandchildren, not 'stepgrandchildren.' No child should be saddled with the term 'step'-anything. They're children, period, and children are born to be loved."

I took Grandpa's words to heart, and have always viewed Tyra and Kevin as the children God wanted me to have and raise. This was my "found family." To Tyra, whose relationship with her biological father ended when she was twelve, I was "Daddy" almost from the start, and on her eighteenth birthday she went to the District Court and had her last name legally changed to mine, then came home and surprised Lynetta and me with the news. My heart was so full, there are no words to describe those feelings. Kenny kept seeing his dad up to his death in 1997.

Then, in 1999, he suddenly stopped referring to me as his stepfather and instead I became "Dad." After all the years of going to his soccer and baseball games, band concerts, and trying to be there for him as well as his sister, I felt Kenny had finally accepted me fully into his heart.

But our story doesn't end there. Three years ago Tyra married a man with three children from a previous marriage. She asked me what I thought about having "stepgrandchildren," and I repeated my grandfather's words to her.

Then Kenny told Lynetta and me that he and his fiancée were expecting and that now we were finally going to have our first "real" grandchild (that is, not acquired by marriage). My wife and I didn't quite know what to respond to his statement; finally I told him that all my children and grandchildren are my "real" offspring, even though I've never been a biological father.

Delilah, it upsets me when I hear people all the time talking about their "stepchildren" and "stepgrandchildren." I want to tell them that children shouldn't be labeled like that—the heart doesn't care who their parents were, only that they are the children God sent to be raised and loved so that when the time comes they in turn will know how to raise and love children of their own. I may not have fathered any children in my lifetime, but I have two wonderful children and four beautiful grandchildren that the love of my life, my wife of twenty years, has given me.

It is more than I deserve, and without her I would cease to exist.

Last year I was diagnosed with a severe heart condition. My youngest grandchild, Sage, is now two years old and starting to talk some. My doctor has said that she "guesstimates" that I will not live long enough to see Sage graduate from high school. She figures that I've got about five or ten years, maximum, to live, as my heart condition cannot be repaired by surgery.

All parents want to leave their children a legacy. I won't be able to leave my children any money, but I'd still like to leave them something. Delilah, you have a national audience, and I'm hoping you'll use your show to get people to drop the "step" label from their children and/or grandchildren and see those kids as a gift from God to be accepted as "real." Maybe you would start a trend that would spread throughout the U.S. and finally the world. The term "stepchild" would become obsolete and removed from our vocabulary. That would be a legacy that anyone would be proud of.

Thank you, Delilah, for allowing me to tell you about my wife, children and grandchildren and to make my appeal. I hope that it will change at least one person's viewpoint.

God bless,

Bobby

"Child of Mine," performed by Carole King.
Songwriters: Carole King and Gerry Goffin.

"Next Time I Fall In Love"

Hi, Delilah,

Here's a story about a couple who took a quarter of a century to get together—but speaking as one of them, it was worth the wait!

When I was only twelve years old, I noticed a very handsome guy mowing my neighbor's yard. Well, that was the beginning of Diane being madly in love with Darren, who was three years older. I followed him around school like a lost puppy. I tried to talk to him but would get so nervous that it felt as if my brain had shut down. After carrying the torch for three years, I finally gave up and started dating other guys. I married someone from high school, it didn't work out and I decided to move to California.

For the first time in my life I felt complete.

I remarried, but after almost five years my second marriage ended, too.

Last September after a conversation at work on "crushes," a co-worker encouraged me to find Darren on the Internet. I decided I would, as a fun and friendly gesture—I had no other agenda whatsoever. Darren had played in a band, and I sent an e-mail to their Web site. I received a response from him two days later. Darren had been divorced for ten years and had a fourteen-year-old son. We continued to e-mail and then to talk on the phone, sometimes several times a day. We became very close friends, and I felt as if I had gone back in time to the "I love Darren" days of my adolescence. But with a difference—this time the feeling was mutual! I moved back to Ohio a couple months ago to be with Darren and his son. I can honestly say, for the first time in my life I felt complete.

I guess those teenage crushes people smile at aren't always just a passing fancy. I knew all along that Darren was the one for me! We are finally together twenty-five years later and couldn't be happier!

Thanks, Delilah.

Sincerely,

Diane

"The Next Time I Fall," performed by Bobby Caldwell.
Songwriters: Bobby Caldwell and Paul Gordon.

"ALL MY LIFE"

Dear Delilah,

Sometimes the love of your life is someone you've known forever—that's my story.

I was born fifty-two years ago this August, and the day my parents brought me home from the hospital as a newborn, I was put into Keath's arms. Keath was only seventeen months older than I, and he was the proverbial "boy next door." An alley divided our property lines, and our parents were best friends. Both families were large, and my brother Randy and Keath became close friends. I followed them everywhere as we were growing up, and at age seventeen I acknowledged to myself that I was in love with Keath.

I got up my courage and blurted out that I had loved him all my life.

Maybe I should have put my feelings on the line, but I had no reason to believe Keath thought of me as anything but a kid sister, and so I never took the risk. I became engaged and married right after high school, and though I didn't see Keath except once, briefly, for more than thirty years, we kept in touch with each other's lives through our families. He, too, married and had children, but both of us ended up divorced. Then, on July 4, 2005, Keath's younger sister Cindy called me and said that Keath would like me to e-mail him.

I felt like I was seventeen again—madly in love with Keath but scared to death that he still thought of me as another kid sister. But this time I decided I would put my feelings on the line. Not immediately—first there were a bunch of e-mails sharing feelings about our lives, our divorces, my becoming a grandmother for the first time, our families. Finally that fall we met for lunch one Sunday. I got up my courage and blurted out that I had loved him all my life, and he responded, "Sondra, I've always loved you, too, and I always will." We've been together ever since.

God is giving us a second chance, and we live every day to the fullest. In May 2005, Keath was diagnosed with lymphoma, but it's in remission for now. I look at every day we have together as a gift from God. Our parents are now deceased, and I know that they're looking down on us and saying, "It's about time you two got it together." Delilah, I would love you to dedicate a song to us. We listen to your show, and you're a great inspiration to us and all your other listeners.

Love,

Sondra

"All My Life," performed by Aaron Neville and Linda Ronstadt. Songwriter: Karla Bonoff.

"No Getting Over You"

Hello, Delilah,

First I'd like to tell you that I listen to your radio show every single night. I really enjoy all the calls you get, and I can relate to the people who are heartbroken, sad or in pain. Been there, done that. My favorite calls are from those who get second chances with the love of their life. I am praying this will happen to me. Here is my story.

In July 2003, I married an air force firefighter who took me to live in another state. I had never been away from San Antonio, or from my family. It was very difficult starting a new life, leaving my job, which I'd had for over fifteen years, and relocating with my seven-year-old daughter. Sad to say, I couldn't take it. After just eleven months of marriage, I left this man and decided to come home.

So I got in the car with my child and started driving. I knew from the moment I got on the road that it had been a mistake to leave, but I couldn't turn back. Too much had already been done—my belongings were being shipped back to Texas, my family was expecting us back in a few days. What else could I do but drive? I never got to see my husband again since he was on temporary duty when I left. I was a coward—I lacked the courage to leave while he was there, so I took the easy way out and left while he was away. We never had any closure, I never saw his face again, never got to feel his arms around me and never even gave him an explanation as to why I left. The thing is, I still loved him.

I never got over him, Delilah, and after searching for him for over two years, I found he had left the country. I obtained his e-mail address and sent him a short note telling him I wished him well and was sorry for the way I had left. He responded, forgiving me, and we started communicating regularly. We talked about everything and anything that had been kept inside for years, and it was clear to both of us that we still had love in our hearts for each other. Now, over three years later, we will be seeing each other again in December for the first time since May 29, 2004. He will be coming to see me, and I admit I am overjoyed, but also scared to death. I don't know what I'll do the moment I see him. Run into his arms, kiss him and never let go? Or break down and shed tears of pure happiness? Can we really work things out and start a new life again? Guess we'll just have to wait and see.

> It was clear to both of us that we still had love in our hearts for each other.

I would like to ask you to please choose a song for me. And please keep up the good, good work you do every day on the radio. Some of us out here live through the music you play, and at times only you offer the promise that things will someday get better.

Thank you, Delilah,

Eva

"No Getting Over You," performed by The Vibrators.
Songwriter: Ian Carnochan.

"Always on My Mind"

Dear Delilah,

My story spans thirty-six years and proves that true love is worth the wait.

Mat and I met as seventh graders in 1971. We were in the same Spanish class, and a flirtation began when I had to pass him some papers and replied "You're welcome" to his "Thank you." My family had just moved back to California from Mexico, and he hadn't realized I spoke English as well as Spanish, but now that he knew, he continued to talk to me. I had a crush on Mat that went on for years, but it wasn't until the tenth grade, in 1974, that we officially became boyfriend and girlfriend.

> If ever a love was meant to be, it's ours.

We were together for almost a year and very much in love, but due to circumstances beyond our control (family and health issues), we split up. We remained good friends at first, but ultimately drifted apart.

After graduation from high school, I left home for Alaska and enrolled at the University of Alaska, Fairbanks. I had heard that Mat was up there, too, but I could never find him. In time I got married to a wonderful man and had two children in Fairbanks. We lived there for ten years and then moved in 1984 to Washington State.

My husband and I attended my tenth high school reunion in 1986, and so did Mat. I danced with him and learned he was also married with two children. After the reunion, I returned to my life in Washington, and had no further contact with Mat.

My husband passed away the year of our twentieth reunion, so I was unable to attend. I didn't know if Mat had attended or not. But I found he was often on my mind. Then, last year, we had our thirtieth reunion, and I was determined to be there. I started hounding everyone I knew to find out if Mat was planning to attend as well. Finally, a dear friend e-mailed me and told that he had "just gotten off the phone with Mat," who was now single, and that he had said "some very nice things" about me—so did I want his phone number?

I was both elated and terrified as I dialed Mat's number, so the message I left on his answering machine wasn't exactly coherent. But he called me back within twenty minutes, so at least my babbling didn't scare him off. We talked a long time that night and continued to talk on the phone over the next few weeks. Then he invited me to meet him in California. We enjoyed our entire weekend together, which was true magic! We realized that we really should have stayed together all along, but that we had become two very wonderful people by being apart.

The amazing thing is that Mat *was* in Alaska at the same time I was—in fact we worked in the same building (the company he worked for was on the top floor and I worked in the basement) at the same time! We also attended the University of Alaska, Fairbanks, at the same time, but had different majors so were in different buildings. He lived on the east side of town, I lived on the west—but our children were born in the same hospital one year apart from each other! Finally, Mat and his family moved to California in 1985, the year after my family left Alaska. He was in Bellingham, a town I lived in for a long time. Coincidence? I think not. Serendipity, more like.

Mat and I were married June 14, 2007, and are moving back to Fairbanks, Alaska, in August. If ever a love was definitely meant to be, it's ours. Delilah, please dedicate a song to us.

Yours truly,
Laurie

"Always on My Mind," performed by Willie Nelson.
Songwriters: Johnny Christopher, Mark James and Wayne Carson Thompson.

"(You're My) Soul and Inspiration"

Hey, Delilah,

Here's a story to encourage any of your listeners who made the same mistake as I did, breaking up with the love of their life. Because twenty-three years later, we're back together!

Woody was my high school sweetheart, but just before my nineteenth birthday, I very stupidly broke up with him. Later I realized it was a mistake, but by then he was gone, and I ended up marrying someone else. That marriage lasted sixteen years, but it never really felt right. More and more, I realized there had only been one relationship that did feel right, and that was with Woody.

I hadn't seen Woody at all during the sixteen years of my marriage, but I hadn't been able to forget him. Sometimes I would think wistfully of what might have been, especially as it became clear my husband and I were headed for divorce court. Then, four months after the breakup with my ex, I was grocery shopping and bent over to get a bottle of soda from the bottom shelf. I saw a pair of legs in men's trousers, looked up—and there was Woody! It was so eerie, as if he had stepped out of a time machine. He didn't seem to have aged at all, and I was glad I had worn a nice outfit to the store that day.

We were both astonished to run in to each other like that after all those years apart. After talking a few moments, we realized we were both single again. Well, we reconnected that very afternoon, and for the next four years, we spent only two nights apart. This time nothing was going to keep us from the altar, and we celebrated our sixth anniversary this past May 19.

> Life doesn't get any better than being married to your soul mate.

When Woody and I touch, it's like two puzzle pieces fitting together. We were meant to be together, and he knows how to touch my very soul. In the fullness of time, we are learning all about each other, slowly but surely. When to give space, when to hug—you know the kind of thing, Delilah. Of course, neither of us is perfect, so we have our ups and downs, but bottom line: the good far outweighs the bad. I feel so blessed to have regained the love I foolishly let go in my youth.

Please play a song for us, Delilah, and I hope my story will help to change some lives, because life doesn't get any better than being married to your soul mate.

Love,

Angie

"(You're My) Soul And Inspiration," performed by The Righteous Brothers. Songwriters: Barry Mann and Cynthia Weil.

"THE BEST IS YET TO COME"

Hi, there, Delilah,

First a compliment, and then the story.

I love to listen to your show. I share your belief that God's sole purpose for us is relationship—relationship with Him and relationship with one another.

Now the story of reunited lovers. Judith and I met in church. In eighth grade, I was rather shy and not good around girls, so I went to youth fellowship as a congenial way to meet some. It worked. I met Judith and we had our first date on New Year's Eve. We dated off and on until we began going steady as juniors in high school. We attended different high schools, but we went to one another's senior activities and were still steadies at graduation. Again in college we were at different schools, but we continued our relationship from a distance. In our sophomore year we became "pinned,"

I decided to revisit that happier past.

a fraternity term for engaged to be engaged. I was a basketball player, and Judith was a Christian education major.

If only I had stayed true to Judith! But temptation intervened, in the form of a cute freshman girl who set her sights on the junior basketball star (me), and I was swept off my feet. I could parry the moves on the basketball court, but women were something else. I'm ashamed to say I dumped Judith in 1964.

Fast-forward to 1991. My marriage of twenty-three years was in its death throes, as I was hearing the call to the pulpit, and my wife, used to my six-figure annual income, was not willing to be a poor preacher's spouse. The marriage had always been difficult, and was further strained by our teenage son's severe emotional problems.

On the last night of a business trip in North Carolina, just before my alarm went off, I had a dream that I was driving down the street when I saw Judith walking in front of the car carrying a bag of groceries. I was in no hurry to confront my poor behavior from 1964, so I began a U-turn to get out of there. From the passenger seat my mother said, "Kenny, you can't do that!" My mother had died in 1982, and I had never dreamed about her or Judith before. In the dream I stopped my U-turn and went back, greeted Judith and began my apologies by carrying her groceries inside for her. There I met her two girlfriends and her three sons.

I woke up, completed my workday and boarded

my plane home. Thirteen hours after the dream it was still as vivid in my mind as it had been when the alarm woke me, so I took out a notepad and wrote everything down. I was in therapy at the time, and I took my dream notes to my next session. After reading the notes to my therapist, I asked, "What does all of this mean?" He said, "What do you think it means?" We concluded that I was seeking to return to a happier time in my life, and a relationship that had been a healthier alternative to my now decaying marriage.

My "homework" from that therapy session was to decide what I was going to do with my new insights. I decided to revisit that happier past. I began my journey back, listing friends from high school and college with whom I wanted to reestablish relationships. But although Judith was at the top of the list because of the dream, I wasn't able to track her down immediately. I did reconnect with others, however, and eventually was told that Judith was somewhere in Texas. By then I was in the process of getting divorced.

Finally, just before Easter 1992, I got Judith on the phone. At first the conversation was awkward, given how we had parted, but still she was friendly. I found out she was divorced and had answered a call to pulpit ministry. She invited me down for Easter, and I brought my youngest son with me for a visit.

Here comes the amazing part, Delilah. Who was with Judith when I got there but the two girlfriends I had seen in the dream, and Judith had two sons, one of whom looked identical to one of the sons in the dream! Judith did not look like the Judith of the dream (the Judith I had known before our breakup) and neither did the younger son, but hey, it's still weird, no? And it gets weirder.

I told Judith about my dream, and she told me that she'd had a miscarriage between the two boys, so that could have been the third son. And then she told me that *she'd* had a dream about me, too. Her dream: she was lying on her sofa crying about her divorce and being a single parent. I came over to her and began to comfort her, saying, "Everything will be all right." She woke up, angry, and said aloud, "All right? Sure, for you everything is all right, with your wife and children up in Wisconsin."

When my son and I left the Sunday afternoon after Easter, Judith leaned in the car window and kissed me goodbye. A whirlwind courtship followed, and we were married on January 2, 1993. Of our five sons (two hers, three mine, all ours), three are married, and a fourth engaged to be married in October of 2008. We have one granddaughter and two grandsons with another expected in April of 2008. Since 1994 Judith and I have both served churches as head pastors.

Delilah, I share this story with you because in 1992 we used to listen to your show together as we were letting our renewed friendship become more than just friendship. I'd like you to dedicate a song to the women in my life—Judith, my daughters-in-law, Sherri, Mary and Hannah, and my granddaughter Jordan. And bless you for your willingness to be so openly Christian in a time when it isn't a popular thing to do.

Love,

Kenny

"The Best Is Yet To Come," performed by Michael Bublé.
Songwriters: Cy Coleman and Carolyn Leigh.

"BLESS THE BROKEN ROAD"

Dear Delilah,

I'm a long-time listener and have always enjoyed hearing the love stories on your show. Now I have one of my own to share.

Traci and I grew up in Florida and were high school sweethearts. Twenty-one years ago we were on a double date with my best friend, David, and I asked Traci to marry me. She turned me down because she had one more year left of high school, and I was going into the army. I was heartbroken, and I never wrote to her after I left to report to duty.

When she came to visit me, I knew I wanted to spend the rest of my life with her.

She stayed in my heart though, and when I was on leave two years later I went to her house hoping to see her again. Her mom informed me that Traci was married, and all my hopes were dashed. I felt as if I'd broken my heart over Traci all over again.

Shortly after that, I was in a helicopter crash while in

the line of duty and lost my left leg. I was in the hospital for more than two years. It was a real hard time for me, and when I look back now, I'm glad Traci said no to my high school proposal, because I had a lot of growing up to do yet.

Fast-forward twenty-one years, to the present. Traci found David—still my best friend—on MySpace and asked him in an instant message if he'd been in touch with me. David told Traci, "I have him on the phone right now." She told me later when she saw those words, her breath was taken away. David gave her my e-mail address, and we started an e-mail correspondence. Traci wrote that she'd been unhappily married for nineteen years, and now she was divorced. She told me she'd thought about me more than I could ever know and had been looking for me for a while now. It turned out we were living only a three-hour drive from each other—I was in North Carolina and she was in Tennessee. When she came to visit me, I knew I wanted to spend the rest of my life with her.

On the night I proposed to Traci, I gave her my original dog tags from the army. She cried like a baby and said she would never take them off. We got married on August 2, 2007. Traci has a son and a daughter from her first marriage, and if it's God's will, we will have a baby of our own. I've never had any children myself, but I have a great relationship with my wonderful stepkids, and I believe that the Lord put Traci back into my life for a reason.

So that's my story, with a fairy-tale ending I never dreamed of, and I'm savoring every minute of my happily ever after. Please dedicate a song to Traci and Mike.

Thanks,
Mike

"Bless the Broken Road," performed by Rascal Flatts.
Songwriters: Jeff Hanna, Bobby Boyd and Marcus Hummon.

"WITH ARMS WIDE OPEN"

Hi, Delilah,

I often listen to you in the night hours. . .usually when I am writing a letter to the man I am completely and totally in love with. It is nice to have a moment to listen to so many wonderful love stories, and it amazes me that you know just what song to pick to go with the emotions. Here is my story about my true love. We had no contact for many years, but I never fell out of love with him.

I'll start my story at the beginning and just hit the highlights. I met Mark in the early eighties at a dance marathon, where he was a DJ for a local radio station. I fell head over heels for this man. We dated for a while and became intimate. He was my first, and the result of our intimacy was a beautiful baby boy, who is now twenty-two years old. Because of circumstance, age and family expectations, Mark never met his son. And we somehow lost each other.

> We had no contact for many years, but I never fell out of love with him.

Like myself, Mark had moved away from the area, but less than a year ago I came back, just in time to spot an obituary of his dad in a local paper, which told me where Mark was now living. I sent him a Christmas card and was surprised to receive a letter back. We have remained in constant contact these last few months. During our "friendship renewal project," we've discovered the feelings we had for each other twenty-two years ago are still very, very strong. In short, we've fallen in love all over again! We will be reuniting as a family this October, and I couldn't be happier!

Please, Delilah, could you play a song for us?

Thank you and God bless,

Wendy

"With Arms Wide Open," performed by Creed.
Songwriters: Scott Stapp and Mark Tremonti.

"Reunited"

Hi there, Delilah,

I listen to you just about every night to calm down
from the daily stress. A while ago you told a story about
a junior high school couple who reunited after many
years apart. I, too, have a reunion romance story to
share.

In December 1969 I was engaged to a man I loved
very much who was in the air force. Things happened,
and we had to go our separate ways. Both of us married
others, and we had no contact for many years. But I
never fell out of love with him. I carried his pictures
in my wallet and for years wore his old dog tags that he'd
sent me. Eventually I put the dog tags in my wallet with the
pictures. Every year on the night of his birthday, I'd go outside and say to the
moon, "Happy birthday, Ed, wherever you may be, and
I'm still in love with you. God, please keep him safe."

When I got a computer in 1997, my (late) best friend

We talked for the
first time in thirty-
seven years for five
and a half hours!

put me on classmates.com. I checked on the site every day trying to find Ed. He finally did join, and I read his bio. I would send him a birthday greeting on the site, hoping he'd reply, but for six years he didn't. I divorced, and when I started my new life (alone) and moved from California to Wyoming, I changed my bio in classmates.com so he could read that I was single. Then I got brave and left my name in his "guest book" section. He saw it and e-mailed me. I replied and we started e-mailing each other several times a day. Then, after two weeks, I asked if I could call him. We talked for the first time in thirty-seven years for five and a half hours! Next thing I knew he asked to come up to see me. That was in January 2006. It was as if time had stood still and the feelings were still there for the both of us. I moved to Texas two months later to be with him. . .and our wedding took place on April 23, 2007!

I enjoy your show very much, Delilah. Please dedicate a song to Ed and me.

All best,

Karen

"Reunited," performed by Peaches & Herb.
Songwriters: Dino Fekaris and Freddie Perren.

"You're In My Heart (The Final Acclaim)"

Hello, Delilah,

My name is John and I have a wonderful story to tell you about how love will always find a way.

My story begins when I was seventeen years old. My family was going up to a resort in Northern Minnesota to see my grandparents, just as we had done for many years—we always went at the same time every year. This year, however, was going to be different, and it would change my life forever.

Debbie and I didn't talk again for years, but we each felt the presence of the other in our hearts.

We arrived on a Friday night. Saturday morning I went to the lake, where I met a beautiful girl named Debbie. Up until that day, I had never given love at first sight even a moment's thought. But when our eyes met, Debbie and I both felt something happen that we can only describe as love at first sight. We talked the whole day, and the next day she left. But to my surprise and delight, she came back the next weekend, and we exchanged phone numbers and addresses.

As we communicated over the next few months, we became so close that we could not stop thinking about each other. I was thrilled when my parents let me go up to stay on her family's farm for the summer. I worked at the farm that whole summer and earned the respect of Debbie's family in the process.

Debbie and I had no doubts in our minds that we were going to be together for life, but fate decreed otherwise. I had always wanted to join the army, and after high school graduation I did that. The plan was that Debbie was going to follow me when I got settled. But she had grown up on her family's farm and was very attached to her home and her people—leaving them was too much for her to handle. Then she met a guy and got married six months later. On her wedding day Debbie called and told me she had just made the biggest mistake of her life.

Well, not to be outdone, I did the same thing myself six months later! Still, it was too late, I thought, for Debbie and me, and I tried to move on with my life. Debbie and I didn't talk again for years, but we each felt the presence of the other in our hearts as we went about our new lives. When I phoned her after six years, to see how she was doing, we still felt a strong love for each other despite the different directions our lives had taken. I had three kids and she had two, so we weren't about to leave our marriages, but we went on this way for another ten years, talking at least once a year, more often every few years.

Then one day, after I'd had a really bad feeling for weeks and couldn't shake it, I called Debbie and she told me that she had fallen into a deep depression brought on by how her life had turned out and the things she wished she could change. She had lost weight, and the depression was affecting her job and her family. We started talking, and simultaneously realized that we were meant to be together! We both had started the divorce process on our own—and now we are together after almost two decades of being apart.

So true love does exist and is still alive today. Thanks for letting me share our story, Delilah. We'd love you to dedicate a song to us.

Thank you,

John

"You're In My Heart (The Final Acclaim)," performed by Rod Stewart. Songwriter: Rod Stewart.

Second Chance at Love

"Love must be learned, and learned again;
there is no end to it."

—Katherine Anne Porter

Although for most of us life is not a fairy tale in which we marry our first love and live happily ever after, the good news is that for everyone there can be a second chance at love—and more chances than two, if needed, as they often are. I believe God created us to love one another, and that He will give us infinite chances to do so. But we aren't always open to the opportunity to love again—when we've been hurt by the loss of a loved one, whether the loss was due to divorce, death, a painful breakup or something else, we often become self-protective and decide we won't love ever again for fear of suffering another devastating wound.

Happily, for most of us hope is ultimately stronger than despair, and we do eventually decide to risk our hearts again and again. The popularity of songs like "Till I Get It Right," sung by Trisha Yearwood, testify to the power of that hope. Another indication of the strength of that yearning for a second chance at love is the fact that the radio soap opera with the greatest number of episodes (7,222, to be exact, aired between 1933 and 1960) was "The Romance of Helen Trent," the story of a thirty-five-year-old widow's quest to love again.

Although I've had three broken marriages, I'm now in a new relationship and once again feeling hopeful about love. I've only known Paul for a year, never lived with him or given birth to his children. I've not been to his school or his old neighborhood. But I know what makes him smile, and what makes him cry. If he were to leave my life today, I would miss him. I would think of him when I saw a pocketknife in the hands of a young boy, or a soldier in a green beret. And I think of Paul every time I see someone on a motorcycle cruising down the highway, enjoying the wide open road and the wind against their face. Because I know Paul, I know these things make him smile, and I know, too, the things that break his heart. It's a risk to get that close to someone, but I've decided it's a worthwhile risk. I feel that we are enriching each other's lives, and I'm glad I decided to love again.

As with Lost and Found Love stories, Second Chance at Love stories encourage us, offering hope and redemption. For many of us, given the choice, starting over with a clean slate and a new relationship seems preferable to renewing a former relationship. Sometimes broken relationships evoke memories too painful to transcend, and we need to create new memories with a new partner. We look to the second chance at love to allow us to be the wiser, more mature, more relationship-ready partner we have become, and often it does, as the following stories illustrate.

It's not only adults who need second chances at love. Children, too, deserve to be loved, and that's why I have adopted seven in addition to my three biological children. Not everyone is fortunate enough to be born to loving, competent parents, and all too many children, in this country and others, are abandoned to the care of strangers who may not be able or willing to provide the love that should be every child's birthright. Adopting such children is part of my life's mission, and I hope many other adults will feel moved to offer a second chance at love to the many desperate children out there who need them. And if you're one of the walking wounded who still won't give *yourself* a second chance at love, let alone a child, may the stories that follow encourage you to change your mind and reopen your heart.

"Suddenly"

Dear Delilah,

I know you don't know me, but I "met" you on the radio about ten years ago. I think you will like my story.

I was married to my first wife twelve and one-half years and had two wonderful children. In the eleventh year of marriage she was diagnosed with a stomach ulcer, but a year later the diagnosis was changed to cancer. She was given six months to live. I asked her if she would like to travel and see the world, but she just wanted to keep spending as much time with me and our children in our normal routines as she could. She used her final months to teach me how to cook, because up till then I only knew how to barbecue. My first wife was so wise and thoughtful—she created a family cookbook of the kids' favorite recipes so I could take care of them when she was gone.

After she passed away in 1987, I tried to put my life back together. I thought the best thing would be to find a mother for my nine-year-old daughter and seven-year-old son. That ended in disaster, so I stayed single for many years as I raised my children.

When the kids grew up, I started dating again, but I soon burned out and began to think I would never find the right person to spend my life with. I'm a commercial pilot, so I decided to fill the void by spending my spare time as a flight instructor. One Saturday I was invited to a wedding, but I didn't know the couple very well and decided not to go. As usual, I just went to the airport and worked. That Saturday afternoon my four o'clock student didn't show up, leaving me with a Saturday night with nothing to do. Suddenly, I decided to go to that wedding after all.

I ran by the local grocery store and got some cash for a wedding present and picked out a wedding card. I headed out to the country to find the beach house where the wedding was being held, but I got lost twice because the roads were not marked. I said to myself, "If I get lost one more time, I'm going home."

Suddenly, I decided to go to that wedding after all.

Fortunately, I didn't get lost again.

I finally succeeded in finding the wedding reception. I went up to speak to the bride, who was talking to this gorgeous blue-eyed blonde with a beautiful smile. The bride introduced us, her eyes met mine and we just danced the night away. Later, we went up on the deck and watched Comet Hale-Bopp streak through the sky. Betty shared with me that she, too, had been married twelve years and had lost her husband to cancer. She then remarried for four years and lost that husband to bypass surgery that went bad.

We dated no one else from that night forward. We lived two hundred miles apart, but that could not separate us. I would make that long drive late at night after a tough day at work—bad weather, flight delays and trying to keep the passengers happy. I would surf the radio trying to get away from the screaming commercials and the rambling DJs. One night, all of a sudden the seek mode on the radio stopped at this beautiful, soothing voice. A voice that instantly calmed me and relaxed me. Then she said, "This is Delilah." What a joy it was listening to you as I drove to see my loved one. The music and stories were great.

Betty and I will be married ten years on November 8, 2007. That night we met at the wedding is still a magical memory of dancing under Comet Hale-Bopp and the stars, and our own wedding took place six months later. We are going to the Biltmore Estate to celebrate our tenth anniversary and see the Christmas decorations and autumn leaves. Please play a ten-year anniversary song for us.

Thanks for everything, Delilah.

Best,

Terry

"Suddenly," performed by Billy Ocean.
Songwriters: Keith Diamond and Billy Ocean.

"Amazed"

Dear Delilah,

I was a party girl in college and got an A+ in social skills—but B's and C's in academics. When I graduated, I continued my carousing until one fateful night when a friend of mine and I went out for a drink. As we were walking, a car stopped in front of us and two men forced us inside at gunpoint. The next hour and a half was the stuff of nightmares. But someone was watching over me that night because, by some miracle, we were let go. I was euphoric. I had been prepared to die and I had lived. That was all that mattered. I stopped caring about the parties, dreams of falling in love, children and marriage. At twenty-two, I had entered adulthood in a brutal way.

Happy in my little apartment, I rebuilt my life and felt satisfied with eating three meals a day and making just enough money to support myself. There were no more fantasies about becoming a movie star. I didn't go out at night and I lost my signature pudge—i.e., thirty pounds. When men talked to me, I was courteous, yet suspicious. People invited me out, but I declined. Going out was too dangerous.

Though traumatized, I began to think soberly about my future and did the best I could. For a long time, the small changes I made were enough.

A decade later, I realized all my friends were getting married. Was I that different from them? Everyone has bad stuff happen to them, I thought, but they move on. Maybe it was time to step out into the world. I decided I had to seriously pursue romance for my own good. So I dated as much as I could. I usually had a decent three-hour window of meeting the man and eating dinner before needing to make my quick escape home. I put on an excellent show, and I didn't get too involved or ask for anything from these gentlemen. I never intended to fall in love.

> I'm amazed at how life can change for the better when you least expect it.

But then I met Jeff. Resigned and content to continue this solitary journey, I prepared for my first sure-to-be dull date with a high school history teacher. It had all the earmarks of a forgettable evening. The problem was, he was pleasant, handsome and fun to talk to. Hooked into easy conversation, I stopped looking at my watch and forgot my nervousness. More than three hours later, we were still walking around Rockefeller Center on the coldest night of the year. That night, I found myself agreeing to go ice-skating with him. . .then hiking, cross-country skiing, traveling and bowling. A year later, I'm astounded at how much time I've spent outside and how much I could possibly love another person. I'm also amazed at how life can change for the better when you least expect it.

This really is a story about the fact that there is always hope. Thanks for letting me share it, Delilah.

All best,

Adriana

"Amazed," performed by Lonestar.
Songwriters: Marvin Green, Chris Lindsey and Aimee Mayo.

"Hopelessly Devoted To You"

Dear Delilah,

Here's a story about falling in love the second time around.

My second husband, an Israeli immigrant named Zvi, which means "Reindeer" in Hebrew, and I had twenty-five blessed years together. It wasn't enough, but that's more years than many couples get to share, and I'm grateful for them. Over the years I've witnessed the shock and grief of friends who discovered that their long-time husbands were unfaithful, and seeing their pain has increased my appreciation of Zvi's fidelity and dedication to our marriage. Not only was he faithful to our vows, but Zvi never forgot my birthday, our anniversary, Valentine's Day or Mother's Day. He was a true romantic, and as a fellow romantic, that was part of what I loved in him.

Zvi proposed to me on our very first date. Flattered yet startled, I said to him, "We both know the pain of divorce, don't you think we should be cautious this time?" Instantly he replied, "I know what I want, but I can be patient until you realize that you want me." From the first, I had all those delicious "falling in love" feelings, but experience had taught me to be cautious and get to know people over the long term rather than acting impulsively.

Ultimately it was his devotion to his children that made up my mind about marrying Zvi. When I met him, he was in the midst of a complicated divorce, and his two children were living in the New York City borough of Queens, while he was in Manhattan, near his workplace. Although their mother had legal custody of the children, she wasn't around much. Zvi was adjusting to a new job and working to the point of exhaustion to support himself and his kids, but he faithfully made the long trip from Manhattan to Queens to visit his son and daughter every Wednesday and bring them to his apartment every weekend, whatever the weather or his energy level. He knew how much his children longed for him, and he longed equally for them. This was, I knew, a man who would take seriously his promises "to have and to hold. . .for richer and for poorer, in sickness and in health, until death do us part."

Ultimately it was his devotion to his children that made up my mind about marrying Zvi.

And he did. He showed the same devotion to me, his wife, and to our own biological child as to my stepchildren, whom he obtained legal custody of before we married. A psychologist who worked with the disabled, he was a devoted advocate for people with disabilities as well.

Zvi died peacefully of a silent heart attack in February 2006. While I held him in my arms when he was unconscious but still breathing, I felt him giving out a silent message—"Only love matters." I try to live by that mantra now, and to be grateful for the many good qualities he passed on to his children—integrity, an affectionate nature, a sense of humor, an inquiring mind, an appreciation of God's creation and love, a love of life and, especially, his devotion to all whom he loved. I am also grateful that each of the three programs where he worked held a beautiful memorial service for him, in addition to his SRO funeral, so his children could understand how special their father was not only to us, but to the many other people whose lives he touched.

Delilah, I'm a big fan of your show—you listen so sympathetically and have a gift for saying exactly the right thing. Please choose a song to dedicate to Zvi, my devoted husband.

Blessings,

Joan

"Hopelessly Devoted To You," performed by Olivia Newton John. Songwriter: John Farrar.

"Heart and Soul"

Hello, Delilah,

I believe God has a great plan for each and every one of us, and my own story is an example of that.

When I was a kid, I would visit my uncle a lot. My uncle had a friend who was seven years older than I was, but although I heard a lot about him, I never once laid eyes on him. We always seemed to just miss each other in our comings and goings from my uncle's house.

Well, I grew up, married an abusive man, had kids, fought cancer and won, and got divorced. Before my divorce was final, I was at my cousin's daughter's birthday party when I finally met my uncle's longtime friend. He was divorced, and we talked for a while about divorce and other things, and I left the party thinking he was cute and easy to talk to, but I didn't expect to see him again anytime soon.

Months went by. I was healing from the cancer, taking care of my kids, and finally getting my divorce. Then I was invited to a baptism party for my cousin's daughter at my uncle's house. I went to the party, not thinking I would see my uncle's friend there, but lo and behold, it turned out he was the baby's godfather. I spotted him sitting alone at a table—which was not like him, he is usually very social. But if he'd been surrounded by people, I probably wouldn't have approached—because he was alone, I did. Our eyes met, and from that moment on, we have not left each other's side.

Clearly, it was God's plan to put this man in my life, but not until we were both free. He arranged it so we didn't meet until it was time to share our lives. We were married on May 26 and are happy as clams. My husband loves my kids as if they were his own, and I have found the best husband in the world. A *true* man, a man who doesn't lay a finger on me and gives heart and soul to his family. He longed for a family and tells me that now he has everything he ever wanted as well. I believe that God sent me my soul mate, and although I went through a lot on the journey, it was all worth it to have him and our family. Please dedicate a song to us.

God bless,

Jenny

> Clearly, it was God's plan to put this man in my life.

"Heart and Soul," performed by The Winans.
Songwriters: J. Dibbs, Marvin Winans, Carvin Winans.

"ALWAYS AND FOREVER"

Dear Delilah,

My story is about finding my "yes" to love through "no"—or getting to an answer backward.

I had just ended a long-term relationship—literally only a few days earlier—when I met Phillip. The breakup had been mutual and amicable, though difficult. They always are. We had both come to the realization that it wasn't "it" and we needed to move on.

Phillip was going to be my distraction. He didn't know any of my other friends—well, the one who introduced us, but that was it—and his presence would help keep me from backsliding into a comfortable past relationship

Sometimes you can find yes through no.

I knew I needed to put behind me. I didn't think I was the kind of person who would really appeal to Phillip, so I didn't feel bad about giving him his assigned jobs of entertainment and companionship—not that I mentioned that to him at the start!

Imagine my surprise when we kept spending time together. My confusion as he actually weathered the fallout from my prior breakup. Things seemed to be happening. Even getting. . .serious. This just wasn't supposed to happen! I needed to explain. My own (eventual) confession was that the order of things was supposed to be: (1) he was the post-breakup guy who couldn't last, (2) I was going to stop renting/stop having a roommate, (3) I was going to buy my own perfect apartment—my very first home—and then (4) explore my options, my life before me, under my control.

Well, I probably framed it as just being "too soon" to get into a new relationship. That I didn't feel ready. That I was supposed to be focused on pulling myself together and figuring things out. All very true! Then he asked me to move in with him.

We were both in our thirties, never married, and he had never asked anyone to live with him before; it was a giant gesture. I didn't know what to say. I had my plans, and they didn't involve living in someone else's home. . . . But he was pretty special.

My own parents had divorced, and I believed in divorce—I don't think people should stay together who don't want to be together, if at all possible. But that meant I had to really, really believe something could work before making a commitment. Living together— especially given the housing market in New York City— was a serious step for both of us.

I didn't know what to do! Was he "the one"? What if it all went south? I'd be out on the street with no equity, no home. My thoughts were in an endless spin cycle, as I tried to figure out some way of knowing, searching for some sign or clue to show me how to decide. How could I know?

And then it seemed so obvious. I thought: *Well, you're not going to turn him down, are you?*

And I realized, no way! I wasn't going to walk away from this man—he was wonderful! So I knew that while I was filled with uncertainties and wasn't at all confident about saying "yes," I was 100 percent certain that "no" was the *wrong* answer. Sometimes you can find yes through no.

This year is our twentieth wedding anniversary, so I'm very glad I figured it out.

Thanks,

Elisabeth

"Always and Forever," performed by Heatwave.
Songwriter: Rod Temperton.

"Second Chance"

Dear Delilah,

I don't know if love conquers all, but I do know it can conquer a lot—in my case that includes aging, a painful past and cancer. Here's my story.

When I met Clark nine years ago, I was fifty-one and had had two failed marriages. I had just gotten my heart broken again and was pretty much finished with love—or so I thought. One night I met Clark in an AOL chat room. There were no sparks or fireworks. . .he was just a nice guy with an interesting screen name. We chatted for a while and said goodbye.

Each time we talked after that, we connected more and more. We started speaking on the phone, and a few months later I went to New Orleans (where he lived) on a visit with my sister and her kids. We met, and Clark showed me around his town. Now there was no denying it—we were in love. And that love only deepened with time.

Eventually Clark moved to Phoenix (where I live), and we married in May of 1999. In August I went to the doctor for a checkup and was diagnosed with stage IIIC ovarian cancer. Ovarian cancer is a disease that has very few symptoms, so by the time it is diagnosed, it is usually advanced, as mine was.

Clark was a bachelor who'd never even lived with a woman before we married, yet he took better care of me than my own mother could have. He went through the whole ordeal with me—the hair loss, the horrible nausea, the overwhelming fatigue—and he pulled me through when I didn't know if I could go on.

Now, eight years later, I remain in remission, and my chances of beating the odds increase with every year that passes. When we celebrate our wedding anniversary, we also celebrate our "second chance" anniversary. A disease that tears many couples apart has only brought us closer.

A few years ago, Clark got his own cancer diagnosis. Prostate cancer has a lower mortality rate than ovarian cancer, but it's still an ordeal. I was grateful to be able to take care of Clark and repay all the love and devotion he showed me during my illness. He is also currently in remission.

So here we are, both relatively healthy and still very

happy. We now have three grandchildren, whom we adore.

I don't know how I would have made it through the cancer if Clark hadn't come into my life and given me a reason to fight. God sent him to me just in time, and I thank Him every day for the gifts of love and life.

Thanks, Delilah, for letting me tell our story, and I hope you can find the perfect song for it.

Best wishes,

Linda

"Second Chance," performed by .38 Special.
Songwriter: Max Carl, Jeff Carlisi, Cal Curtis.

"FAMILY AFFAIR"

Dear Delilah,

I'm in my late fifties and I have a quirky love story
to share with you, about the man I'll be marrying on St.
Patrick's Day.

Our family tree is so twisted and entwined that I
fondly refer to it as "the family bonsai." I have remained
close to my sister's former husband, Bill, and am "Aunt
Carol" to the children of his wife of four years, Lynn. Lynn
and I are as close as sisters—we e-mail back and forth
every day, and frequently talk on the phone. Lynn has
three wonderful grown children with children of their
own, and Bill has two children, my niece and nephew,
John and Amy, who also have children. I have a son, Scott.

Lynn and her ex-husband, Steve, still have a cordial
relationship and continue to include each other in
family gatherings. I have known Steve for four years;
we have become acquainted via family parties and he
has been at my house for Christmas Eve the past three
years and at my son's for Thanksgiving for the past four
years. His daughters and I are best of friends. One
December night when my housemate declined to go to
a family party with me, I had a chance to spend some
one-on-one time with Steve. . .to really talk, to share
a kiss in the driveway. . . .wow! That night changed my

life forever. Suddenly I was in love! Delilah, I adore this man—I'm the lady in St. Mark's Square on TV shouting to the pigeons and everyone who will listen. And Steve feels exactly the way I do.

> Love comes along when you least expect it.

It gets better. These two madly in love fifty-somethings who have been standing in front of each other all these years will tie the knot in just seven weeks. And the first person everyone will see coming down the hall at the little winery lit by candles on St. Paddy's Day night will be Steve's ex-wife, my "sister" Lynn, followed by my best friend Miriam, and then me. . .escorted by the husband of Steve's ex-wife and the ex-husband of my sister, Bill.

My story shows how love and fun and a true sense of what it means to be part of a wonderful extended family can lead to a magical storybook romance. Please dedicate a song to Steve and me, Delilah, and remind all your listeners that love comes along when you least expect it.

Many thanks,
Carolyn

"Family Affair," performed by Sly & the Family Stone.
Songwriter: Sylvester "Sly Stone" Stewart.

"Listen to Your Heart"

Hello, Delilah,

I have a story to tell you about getting a second chance at love.

I was in a very bad relationship in Oklahoma, where I had lived with a man for nine years. I had loved him and put heart and soul into the relationship, but five years earlier he had started to get abusive. I knew I should leave him, but I just couldn't bring myself to do that.

On November 23, I went alone to Tennessee to spend Thanksgiving with my family. During my visit, I felt I was getting signs telling me I needed to leave Oklahoma and start a new life on my own, but I had never been on my own before, and I was afraid. On November 28, I boarded a plane to return to Oklahoma, and when I got to my seat a man bent over a laptop was in the seat next to mine. During the flight, I found my gaze constantly drawn to him, but when he'd look up, I would look away. Once I wasn't quick enough though, and our eyes met— and suddenly there were all those fireworks and "love at first sight" feelings. We talked for the entire flight, and he told me he actually had a first-class ticket (yes, he showed it me), but something had told him to sit in the seat next to mine even though there was no one in the neighboring seat at the time.

We had exchanged phone numbers on the flight, and when I got home, we called each other regularly and talked for hours. Truly, this man was my soul mate. Finally I moved to Chicago two days before the new year to start a new life. So far, it is working out beautifully. This man cares about my happiness. On the plane I had told him of my dream to see the ocean, and for Christmas he surprised me with a trip to Key West. I had the time of my life.

> Suddenly there were all those fireworks and love-at-first-sight feelings you read about but never think will happen to you.

I think it was your show in Oklahoma that gave me the courage to make one of the scariest moves I have ever made. I have heard you talk about the need to follow your heart, and that's what I did. It is the best move I have ever made. I have a great job and a wonderful man in my life. Please play a song to celebrate my new life and new love, Delilah.

Love,

Jennifer

"Listen to Your Heart," performed by Roxette.
Songwriters: Per Gessle and Mats Persson.

"Taking You Home"

Dear Delilah,

Here's a love story with a happy ending.

Phil and I met the summer of 2005 while we both worked nights at a hospital. His hot-dog cart had been set up outside my switchboard office as an experiment in offering real food to the third shift. For months we chatted in between my calls and his customers. He would leave at 1:00 a.m. and I'd go back to my board. In the wee hours of the morning, I'd find myself praying, "God, please send a man like Phil into my life." I wondered why I never met a guy like Phil to date.

> He said that I was the woman he had always dreamed of meeting but thought couldn't exist.

When the hospital ended the food experiment, Phil and I exchanged phone numbers. I figured he was just being polite, and we'd never talk to each other again. But *much* to my surprise, he called early in December and asked me out. I was a wreck! And I had never been nervous before about dates. We spent a wonderful weekend in the mountains, and we parted with me happily anticipating hearing from Phil again soon.

I didn't hear from him all through the Christmas season. What a horrid few weeks that was! I finally resigned myself to the idea that he had no further interest. When the phone rang, I stopped expecting or even hoping it would be him.

Then he called.

We began dating regularly in January of 2006. One evening, he played a Don Henley song and said it described how he felt. He said that the weekend in the mountains, he realized that I was the woman he had always dreamed of meeting but thought couldn't exist. It rather overwhelmed him, and that's why he took so long to call again.

We've both been married before, and Phil had previously decided he would never marry again. But as Gracie Allen said, you shouldn't put a period where God put a comma. He proposed to me in January of 2007, and we'll be married in a park next to a waterfall on May 10, 2008. I firmly believe that God—using Chicago-style hot dogs (hey, why not?)—brought us together. I'm so blessed, and so happy.

Please play a song for all the couples who have been or are discouraged, thinking it'll never happen to them. And for all the couples who have had their own miracles.

Thanks, Delilah!

All best,

Jaci

"Taking You Home," performed by Don Henley.
Songwriters: Stuart Brawley, Don Henley and Stan Lynch.

"Never Alone"

Dear Delilah,

I have listened to your show for years, and I want to share my story with you because *you* are the reason my life got turned around on two separate occasions.

At thirty-six, my life went into a downward spiral. After years of frustration and heartbreak with fertility problems, I finally became pregnant, only to learn it was an ectopic—doomed—pregnancy. During my recovery from emergency surgery, I discovered that my husband was having an affair. Two days after I confronted him about it, this man I had thought I would grow old with asked for a divorce. Devastated, I moved back home, where I still had family, to start picking up the pieces.

> He not only tells me he loves me but shows me in everything he does.

But I found no safe haven at home, where my mother's alcoholism had escalated, straining her marriage to my stepfather. I had realized from the time I was fourteen that my mother secretly drank behind closed doors. Some days she was functional, but others not—now the functional days were few and far between as she was drinking more than ever.

During this time I started having numbness, loss of movement in one arm and blindness in my left eye. At first I dismissed these as the side effects of stress. But when the symptoms worsened, I consulted a specialist. After many painful tests, including a spinal tap, I was diagnosed with multiple sclerosis. There was no one for me to lean on—my mother was drinking herself to oblivion because she couldn't cope with her own life, and my stepfather was overwhelmed by living with an alcoholic. I tried to be brave and tell myself I could deal with this on my own, but I couldn't. The burning, numbness and paralysis—and the anticipation of even worse—took their toll. I decided I would be better off and less of a burden if I ended things now.

One evening I took my stepfather's gun and sat on the floor listening to your station, summoning up the nerve to blow my brains out. Then a story about a woman who was completely paralyzed came on. She had no use of any of her limbs, but she saw life as a gift and felt blessed every day. Delilah, listening to that story I felt ashamed of myself. I had a lot more than that woman, but instead of counting my blessings, I was sitting on the pity pot and preparing to make more grief for those who loved me. How could I be so selfish? I had MS, but did I have to let MS have me? I put down the gun and began my battle with MS, a battle in which I have the control, not the disease.

I am proud to say that I started treatment, my symptoms improved and I am living a productive life. My mother went into rehab and already has nine months' sobriety, which is also a great thing for her marriage. For my birthday in February, my grandmother gave me a subscription to eHarmony.com. She had listened to you praise their success and talk about how many people found the love of their life online. At first, I was horrified by my grandmother's gift. The idea of meeting someone online was scary. But then I met Scott (yes, I am the writer of the e-mail you read in your commercial for eHarmony).

At our first meeting, I noticed immediately that Scott had wonderfully kind eyes and a voice that was soft and soothing. The very day we met I told him about the MS. I figured if my illness was going to make him run, better to get it over with. He never flinched. He wanted to know all about the disease and what he could do for me. Our first meeting and he was already asking what he could do to help! I later learned that after we separated that day, he went to the library and checked out every book he could find on MS. Since we began dating, I have had some flare-ups, but Scott has been at my side battling through every one of them with me.

Delilah, Scott is the most incredible man—kind,

wonderful, giving—and even with full knowledge of my illness, he says he wants to spend a lifetime with me. I had always heard of soul mates but never understood what that meant before. Under Scott's positive influence, I bounce back from every physical trial and never let myself give up. Every night I go to sleep feeling blessed by his love. He not only tells me he loves me, but also shows me in everything he does. He is Mr. Romance. Oh, and did I mention that he is gorgeous, plus he cooks and does laundry? And to think I might have committed suicide and never met this man!

Delilah, I just want to thank you for saving my life, not once, but twice. You give hope to the hopeless, love to those who feel unloved and, most important, a venue to let us know we are never alone.

There are so many wonderful songs that you play. As Scott and I plan our future together, we ask that you find the mushiest love song to play for us. This is a love that will last a lifetime. And thank you again for being such a huge part of making this happen. . .even though you didn't know a thing about it.

Devotedly yours,

Kelli

"Never Alone," performed by Jim Brickman and Darrell Brown. Songwriters: Gary Burr, Sarah Buxton and Victoria Shaw.

Letting Love Go

'Tis better to have loved and lost
than never to have loved at all.

—ALFRED, LORD TENNYSON

Letting love go is probably the hardest thing we ever have to do in life. Accepting the loss of a loved one—whether the cause is death, divorce or renunciation—is always painful, as many songs attest, including "Letting Love Go," performed by Everything But the Girl, and Bonnie Tyler's version of "Total Eclipse of the Heart." And the enduring popularity of Mark Dinning singing "Teen Angel" suggests that we find it especially unacceptable to lose a loved one whose life was cut off prematurely.

I know firsthand how hard it is to let love go, and I'm not sure we ever really do. When I met my first husband, George, I was swept away in an instant in an emotional river that was wilder than Oregon's Rogue River. Turbulent and troubled, the relationship we had was powerful and destructive. And as young and passionate as I was, I found myself washed out to sea without a safe vessel to bring me back to shore. When we parted ways after only a few years, I managed to stay afloat long enough for the Lord to wash me ashore like a piece of broken driftwood, and there I lay unable to function for quite some time.

When I tried to begin again, to find my feet and walk, I didn't know what to do, I was still so terribly in love with George. Friends, my mother, my pastor, a counselor—even complete strangers—told me to "move on." I tried, but the feelings were still there.

I even clung to my love for George after our divorce was final. When he moved to a new city, I went on a "vacation" with our baby son to the same city and looked him up. George seemed pleasantly surprised by our appearance, and I deceived myself into thinking the marriage wasn't over after all, that we would reconcile and live happily ever after just the way I'd thought when we got married. One morning I walked into his bathroom and saw what I thought was a sign that we were meant to be: a brass key chain engraved with my pet name for George. It was only when I turned over the key chain and saw the words "All my love, Enid" that I faced reality and ended both the "vacation" and the pipe dream that George and I would ever be reunited.

But even though I knew intellectually that it was over, I still wasn't over George in my heart. For the next twenty years I tried to figure out how to stop loving him. I had the notion that if I were to give my heart to another, I would stop loving him. Or that if I truly loved another, I could not still love George. That there was something terribly wrong with me if I was involved with someone but could not stop feeling a connection to my firstborn's father.

And then one day, I met a man who took my breath away. Faster and harder than I fell for George, I fell for Michael. And for the first time in over twenty years, my heart returned to its place in my chest, and I went to sleep without wondering where George was and if he was well and safe and warm. Actually, that's a bit of an overstatement. I still wonder about him, still hope and pray that he is experiencing a good life and that he is loved. But I no longer feel a terrible ache in association with that love.

God did not intend for me to be connected to Michael the way I had hoped we would be, and instead I have had to learn to be content with a kinship, a bond that others may not understand, but is a lovely thing in my life. And because of that bond, and our unconditional love, I have learned so very, very much.

Mostly I've discovered that the love that lives within the human heart isn't like a computer file that can be deleted when it is no longer convenient. It doesn't go away when you decide it's time to "move on." It isn't something that you can control or wish or pray away.

Paul, the gentle, loving man I am involved with today, cried one night, remembering Karen, the woman he loved in high school, the woman who has been in his heart ever since. He felt he should have stopped loving her, was afraid that I would feel bad knowing that he still loved her, still wondered if she ever got over the heartache he had caused when she was young and vulnerable. I held his hand as he cried. I didn't feel threatened or jealous—I felt only compassion for him and for her. Because I know firsthand that when you love someone deeply, and you are allowed the privilege of entering their soul, you never really stop loving them. You might never see them again, but the knowledge of their essence is with you forever. I hope that Paul is able to find Karen one day, and let her know what an impact she had on his life, and how he cherished her memory like a golden treasure. I felt as if I had witnessed something close to sacred when I witnessed him mourning that love of long ago. And I hope Karen can forgive Paul for the wounds caused by his teenage foolishness, knowing that he loved her wholeheartedly and that her memory sustained him during years of a miserable marriage and warmed his heart during the dark nights of his life.

I've heard it said that intimacy means "into me see". . .or "see into me." See into my heart, see into my soul. If this is the essence of real love, why do we think or teach others that love will ever fade or go away? If you really love someone, you know them. You know their hopes and their dreams and their fears. If they are no longer your lover, your husband, your wife, your best friend, do you forget what you know of them? Will I ever forget that George loved to eat hot links with scrambled eggs for breakfast? Will I ever forget that my mom's eyes flashed a deeper green when she was laughing at her own jokes or thinking of something silly? Will I ever forget the songs that she sang when she stood at the sink washing dishes? Or the way her huge hand felt on my feverish forehead when I had pneumonia?

And as time passes, will I forget what the man I thought I would spend my life loving sounded like when he thought he had hurt my heart? Will I forget the taste of his tears when I hurt his? Although convention says I should "get over" him, that I should stop loving him since he is already committed to another and I now have another man in my life, is there any way to stop knowing a person once you know them that deeply?

Even though our hearts and memories don't let go of those we truly loved, there are times we have to let go physically, especially when the loved one dies. The Song of Solomon tells us that "Love is strong as death," and some of these stories suggest that love is actually stronger than death, that our loved ones can and do communicate from beyond the grave.

Whatever the circumstances in which we have to let go of loved ones, the important thing is never to let go of Love. By that I mean that no matter how badly we've been hurt, whatever we've done or whatever's been done to us, it's a mistake to close off our hearts and refuse to love again. A particular person may not want your love at this point in time, but I'm sure that at least ten others do. To deny them is to deny yourself and to deny the loving nature God gave you. I was deeply impressed with a speech I once heard given by a man named Mike McKorkle. The essence of it was this: "In the end God will ask you two questions—what did you do with Me and what did you do with the people I put in your life? He'll want to know if and how you loved them." Ever since I asked God for a sign that He existed and found a Bible tucked under my windshield inscribed "Jesus loves you," I've known He calls me to love Him and all the people in my life. I hope these stories will convince you to do the same, and that no matter how many loved ones you lose, you'll never let go of Love.

"I'll Always Love You"

Dear Delilah,

I'm writing to share with you a story about letting go of love.

I was raised without religion. My Catholic mother and Jewish father both felt they were forced into organized religion as children, and they were determined not to do the same to me. However, I've always considered myself a very spiritual person, and it was that connection with spirituality that led me to volunteer in the respite tent for the recovery workers at Ground Zero in the months after September 11, 2001.

While I was cleaning off the tables in the dining area one day, I met TJ, a handsome, charming fireman with a twinkle in his eye that hid a great deal of pain, sorrow and guilt. It took me quite some time to agree to go out with TJ, but I finally did, after his stint at Ground Zero was over and he had gone back to his firehouse full-time. It became clear after several dates that we had something truly special, and I pushed to the back of my mind any concerns I had about the fact that TJ was a devout Catholic and desperately wanted to raise his children Catholic. I, on the other hand, wasn't even sure I wanted children, and certainly hadn't considered what I would do about religion if I ever became a parent.

It was a rocky road for a while. TJ had terrible survivor's guilt about his colleagues who had died on 9/11—especially about a close friend who had been covering for TJ that day. Our relationship hit an impasse—he was unable to connect emotionally—and I realized that he needed professional help in order to cope with his guilt. I told him we couldn't see each other anymore unless he started talking to someone, and he surprised me by stepping up to the plate and doing just that. Time went by and we got closer and closer—I moved to his neighborhood so we would no longer have to travel for over an hour to see each other.

> I think of him regularly, and I wish him every happiness in the world.

Finally, after two and a half years together, we began to have conversations about marriage.

I was hoping against hope that we could figure out a way to manage our spiritual differences. We always ran into trouble when we talked about kids. Would we have them? Could he raise them Catholic without my participation? Would he be okay with sending them to public school instead of Catholic school? As you might imagine, these conversations were agonizing. It finally dawned on me—after a discussion that ended in tears for both of us—that Catholicism was a hugely important part of his identity and it was unfair to ask him to go through life without being able to share it with his partner. He seemed mostly convinced that we could figure it out, but I could see only the ways in which our spiritual differences would present stumbling blocks for us in the future, leading us to feel inadequate for each other at crucial moments. The crisis came when TJ pressed the issue and asked me to marry him, and I simply couldn't say yes—it didn't feel right. And so we ended our relationship. It was a slow and painful breakup, and I will be sad about it for the rest of my life.

I think of him regularly, and I wish him every happiness in the world. I hope that he will find a woman who believes what he believes, and who wants to build a family with him, because he deserves that. He will be an amazing husband and a wonderful father—I just know it.

Thanks, Delilah,

Amy

"I'll Always Love You," performed by Whitney Houston.
Songwriter: Dolly Parton.

"Bridge Over Troubled Water"

Dear Delilah,

I know you are a Christian, and I want to share with you a story about how God has worked in my life. I am a truck driver and listen to you all the time when I'm on the road at night.

My story begins in 1995. When my sons were in elementary school, they became friendly with a boy I'll call Manny. Manny was born in Germany to German parents. His mother came to the United States when he was four years old with an American military man. As a result Manny's biological father lost contact with his son and had no way of locating him. Manny's mother had family in Germany, but they wouldn't tell Manny's father or other paternal family members where he was.

When Manny was in the fourth grade, his family moved to a different town and he lost touch with our boys. Several years later, around 2003, they reconnected with Manny, now fourteen, at the local county fair. Our sons had livestock showing in the local fair, and Manny was showing horses. They became friends again, and we found out he lived only about three miles from us. On several occasions Manny rode his horse over to our home to visit.

Manny was a typical teenage boy, full of beans and "'tude." Since my wife, Cindy, and I have raised three sons, we could make Manny feel right at home. On several occasions, Manny confided in me that he had endured a rough childhood of physical and mental abuse. He often talked about wanting to get out of his mother's house, but was concerned about leaving behind his siblings.

Manny and I discussed his options, and repeatedly he said he thought his best option was to come live with us. I told him as long as he observed the household rules, he would always be welcome in our home. And on April 9, 2005, his mother appeared at our house and asked us to take him in; she could no longer handle the situation with Manny and his stepfather. Two days later, sixteen-year-old Manny moved in with us.

When he walked through our front door, Manny was carrying an old teddy bear dressed in baby clothes. He told us that his biological father in Germany had given him this bear, and the clothes were his baby clothes. Manny still slept with that bear almost every night. He often said that after he graduated from high school he wanted to go to Germany to find his father. His mother refused to tell him anything about her first husband.

Manny settled smoothly into our household routine, and we came to think of him as a member of our family. Even though Manny wasn't our biological son, we agreed to adopt him, but for legal reasons, we had to wait until he turned eighteen.

Manny was a strong-willed young man, very dedicated to physical fitness, sports and taking care of his body. He had dreams one day of becoming a personal trainer and/or boxer. One of his boxing idols was Muhammad Ali. Manny played football and wanted to wrestle. He also had a part-time job working on a horse farm to make money for his car. But he found time to fall in love for the first time, with a young lady by the name of Kayla. They seemed to suit each other to a T, and it was good to see this troubled young man finding happiness and setting goals for his future.

Through losing our son, we have gained a whole new family.

In November of 2005 I had to spend a week in the hospital. Manny's car had broken down, and he needed a way to get to work and school. Manny had a good friend named Matthew who worked at the same horse farm and attended the same school. We agreed to let Manny stay with Matthew while I was in the hospital. I got out of the hospital on November 8th and talked to Manny on my way home. He was going to spend the night with Matt and then come home after school the next day.

On November 9th, our lives changed forever. Manny and Matt were going back to Matt's house after work to clean up for school when Matt went through a stop light and drove under a semitrailer. Both young men lost their lives that morning. Cindy and I were heartbroken; we had lost a son. Even when you have faith, as we do, it is hard to accept that God has called home such young men, with their whole lives before them.

The day after the boys died, I had to go to the police station and clean out the car they had died in—one of the hardest things I have ever done. Cindy and I found a poem in Manny's book bag that he wrote in February 2004 titled "He Cares." The poem opens, "Why is everyone scared to die, when there is so much love in the sky?" My wife read this aloud, and we just looked at each other and cried. I knew this day that I would see Manny again in heaven.

On Sunday, November 13, 2005, we buried our son. I found out from the minister that in January 2004 Manny had spent the night at a local church at a teen event and had accepted Christ as his savior. Afterward, he wrote the poem "He Cares," which my oldest son read at Manny's funeral. The next day, after

Matt's funeral, my wife and I went back to the school to get the rest of Manny's things. The school secretary seemed very anxious. She said, "I've just been talking to Manny's father." I shook my head. How could that be? Manny's father lived in Germany, and no one knew how to reach him or even who he was. But before we left the school that day, he called again, and I talked to Manny's father for the first time. It seemed that after Manny's death his mother had contacted her family in Germany and gave them permission to contact Manny's father.

Talking to Manny's dad, I could tell the boy had been a lot like his father. Then I asked Manny's dad if he had ever given his son any stuffed animals as a child. "A teddy bear," he told me. I began to cry as I told him that I had his bear, and invited him to come get it and take it home to remember his boy by.

In March 2006 seven members of Manny's German family, including his dad, came to America for the first time to meet some of his friends and visit his final resting place. I met them at the airport with that teddy bear. I believe that God put it all together for a reason. I was able to assemble a picture album with photographs of Manny from the time he came to America until the day before he died. We had the privilege to spend a week with Manny's family and share photos, videos and personal experiences with them. Through losing our son, we have gained a whole new family, truly wonderful people, with whom we maintain regular contact. I just know that God put Manny in our home to be sure that when He took him home his earthly family in Germany would have something to remember him by. And they do.

Thank you so much, Delilah, for being such a solid inspiration to so many. I love every moment I get to listen to you, and hope to hear you play a song for Manny and his German kin. God bless you and keep you safe.

Love,

Doug

"Bridge Over Troubled Water," performed by Simon & Garfunkel. Songwriter: Paul Simon.

"You Are Everything"

Dear Delilah,

Some stories don't end as happily as we would like, but through it all, I have hope. I was engaged, my life was perfect, I couldn't have been happier. . .until my cell phone rang at 11:30 at night and on the other end of the line was a woman who was claiming to be my fiancé's wife! I was shocked, scared, heartbroken. I told myself there was some mistake, that this sort of thing didn't happen to people like me.

Well, sure enough, the man I loved—the man I had given my heart and soul to—had lied to me for over a year. You see, it was a long-distance relationship—he lived two hours north of me and would drive down on the weekend. I never had a clue about the wife. Could I really have been so blind? Even today I don't know how he lived such a lie.

Understandably, this past year I have become very cynical. I started to believe that there is no such thing as a soul mate. But today I changed my mind on that. I work in health care, and today I watched as an elderly man sat quietly with his wife, who had just passed away. I put my hand on his shoulder and asked if there was anything I could do for him. He looked up at me, and with tears in his eyes said, "She was my life, my everything." I didn't know what to reply. I came home from work and cried. I cried for all the pain I had locked up inside of me, for the betrayal I had endured, for my broken heart, and I cried because I had almost given up on the belief that true love does exist. But this frail old man who had just lost the most important person in his life rekindled my faith. God works in mysterious ways,

Someday I will have someone in my life who is my everything. The man I loved had lied to me for over a year.

and while I don't understand, I have been reminded today to trust in Him and that someday I will have someone in my life who is my everything.

Will you please play a song to reinforce that hope, as a reminder that no matter how hard the path is, we will soon be given what God wants us to have.

Thank you, Delilah, and God bless,

Allison

"You Are Everything," performed by The Stylistics.
Songwriters: Thom Bell and Linda Creed.

"I Can Only Imagine"

Dear Delilah,

This story will bring you to tears. I found my true love, only to lose him again.

I was thirty-one years of age and thought that love had passed me by. All my life I had longed for a family of my own, but now I had given up the hope of finding the someone meant for me and having children with him. But maybe I hadn't completely given up, because I couldn't seem to pull myself off Match.com. And that's where I saw him one day. He had sent me an e-mail introducing himself, and when I saw his picture I knew he was The One.

There were a few bumps along the road to love. For starters, I saw Tim on Match.com but couldn't contact him because I wasn't actually a member yet. Frantically I looked through my purse but couldn't find my credit card—I had lost it. I was crushed! This was my someone, I just knew it. Two weeks later my card was found, and the very first thing I did was to purchase a membership on the site and e-mail him.

Tim responded and soon we were talking every day through e-mails and sometimes on a messenger service. Although only thirty-two, Tim was almost completely deaf—he wore a hearing aid, but phone conversation wasn't easy for him. Still, I loved hearing his voice; it wasn't any different because he was hearing-impaired, just a little deeper.

Our first date was on Valentine's Day 2004. My prince was no frog! He was everything I knew he'd be, and I was head over heels in love at first sight. The beauty part is that Tim was, too. That night we started out at a party for the elderly and disabled (my work), then dinner at Applebee's, and finished the night off driving around getting to know each other. We didn't want the date to end. I went home that night knowing that Tim and I would be married and we were. We were planning a fall wedding, but in June I found out I was pregnant. It was the happiest moment of my life. I had truly given up on such a gift. We decided to move up the wedding date, to August 28, 2004.

And so began our all-too-brief happily ever after. Just before our marriage, we'd learned that a rare heart defect that Tim had been born with had become very severe. His heart, now enlarged, had a hole in it, was upside down and on the wrong side of his chest, and his ventricles were switched. Tim and I were crushed. Had we found love only to lose it so soon? Then a beam of hope. One doctor told us about a surgery to correct some of the defects so Tim could live. The surgery was scheduled to be done after the baby was born in February, but Tim's heart monitor indicated trouble.

The doctors said we couldn't wait any longer, so the surgery took place in December. Stress sent me into preterm labor, and bed rest was recommended, but I couldn't do that. I had to be there for Tim. He came through the surgery fine, but a few days later crashed and had to have two more emergency surgeries. We spent our first and only Christmas together in the hospital.

> Had we found love only to lose it so soon?

Several times before our child was born, Tim was on the brink of death and then rebounded. Once he collapsed in my arms at the doctor's, and as they went into CPR, I heard one of the doctors say they had lost him. I asked God for a miracle. Then I phoned some family members and asked them to call their prayer lines, and when I returned to the room, Tim was back with us. God listened and He moved. Tim was transferred to his doctor's hospital, where he flatlined twice more. My whole body shook from fear and disbelief. I had called his family and mine, and for the rest of the night we waited while he was in another emergency surgery.

On February 3rd our baby girl was born. I was

exhausted and very ill from gall bladder disease. Tim was in a coma. My heart had never felt such great joy and such great sadness at the same time. Our daughter was the most beautiful being in the world, and she looked just like her dad. I ached because he wasn't there with me to see our precious Maddie Grace, and I didn't know if he ever would be. Tim underwent a fourteen-hour-long surgery the very next day, the longest day of my life so far. A couple of weeks later he woke up from his coma, and it was a struggle to get him off of the ventilator. Every time we tried, he crashed. He was disoriented, and even asked me who God was.

On Valentine's Day 2005 (the first anniversary of our first date), I got approval to bring our little girl into his ICU room so that Tim could see her for the first time. Holding our baby in my arms, I said, "You wanted to know who God is, Tim. Look at our daughter, Maddie Grace, and you'll understand who God is and what He's done in our lives."

Tim got better, and two rehabs later, in April, he was able to come home. I was so happy, so excited. Finally we were on our way to starting our new lives with our new baby! Tim was even able to go back to work for a few weeks, and things were almost back to normal. We took lots of pictures every day of him and Maddie Grace. She was starting to get used to her dad, laughing at him all the time, which tickled Tim. It wasn't exactly the way I had dreamed our lives would be, but I was so thankful for what we had.

We didn't have it long. By end of May, Tim's only hope was a heart transplant, and his heart gave out for the last time before that could happen. I can't describe in words what it felt like to lay my head on his body and pray his spirit away. We had only been married for eleven months, and we had a beautiful new baby girl. How was I supposed to say goodbye?

Seven months later I'm still struggling with that, Delilah. I've returned to my hometown with Maddie Grace. I just couldn't bear to stay on the beautiful farm in Versailles, Kentucky, that Tim loved so much. I left a piece of my heart there with Tim's memory. I know he still lingers about the place. I think about him all of the time and ache for what he is missing out on. Our daughter has just turned one, and she is the spitting image of her daddy. Maddie Grace is my blessing. Without her, I just don't know where I'd be.

Earlier in this story I mentioned that Tim got to come home for a few months in April. He already had plans for another baby, but I wasn't on board with that. During one discussion, I teased him that we could have one if he would carry it. Very seriously he looked up at me and said, "Chassy, you never know what God has in store for us." Two months later he died. Those words of Tim's never leave me. You really don't know what is in store for you, but you need to be ready for whatever it is. One thing I do know: True love does exist. I found it once and carry it with me every day.

Thanks for letting me share, Delilah.

God bless,

Chastity

"I Can Only Imagine," performed by Angel Me.
Songwriter: Bart Millard.

"Someone To Watch Over Me"

Dear Delilah,

July 10th will be the twentieth anniversary of the day I met the most influential man in my life. Steve became the man all "love interests" were measured against. Most failed miserably.

We were a case of opposites attracting—I was a small-town country girl and Steve a big-city "man" (not much older than me, actually) when I met him at the tender age of sixteen. It was a hot, humid Kansas summer, and Steve was so dazzling and exciting compared to the country boys I grew up with. He was polished, suave, stylish, handsome, intelligent, funny and a lot more sophisticated than I was. My parents were completely hostile to him, which made him even more appealing to me.

This wasn't just "love at first sight" or "first love." Sure, there was that jolt of electricity when we first met, touched, kissed—but there was so much more. We lived three hours apart and spent most of our time on the phone or writing letters to each other, with occasional meetings. Over time our feelings intensified—I knew even as a teenager that this was no passing infatuation.

By December, my parents put their foot down, and I had to end the relationship. Still, not a day passed that I didn't think about Steve. He was always in my mind and in my heart.

On my first day of college, a wonderfully familiar face appeared across the classroom from me. . .Steve! But though I was now free to live my life as I wanted, Steve had married. We spent two years avoiding each other in class and at school functions. Eventually, I was able to talk to him and his wife socially. I couldn't help being a little envious of her, but I tried to tell myself that at least she was making him happy.

Seven years passed. Steve and his wife moved, I married someone else. But sometimes the heart wants what the heart wants, and will not be happy until it gets just that.

My marriage ended, and the desire to find Steve again consumed me. Yet I couldn't bring myself to be a home wrecker in his marriage by calling him. Finally I called his brother and learned that Steve's wife had left him at almost the same time that my husband had left me.

The first time I heard Steve's voice after eleven years, I was sixteen again. We spent four days talking on the phone for hours before he showed up on my doorstep. That first hug from him after so many years apart was absolute heaven.

Steve moved home within two months, and our life together seemed like a dream come true. Two weeks out of the month, his four-year-old daughter stayed with us, and she and I bonded as well. For once, my life seemed perfect. But after only eight months together, our perfect little world crumbled. Steve had been hiding a drug and alcohol problem, and I quickly learned that an addict will do anything for the next fix. He moved out and moved on, taking his daughter—my sweetie—and my love with him.

He always told me he would be watching over me.

Alone again, my past, present and future shattered, I wanted to die. I am a survivor though, and I put one foot in front of the other for three more years. Then I felt a need to find Steve again, but this time it was too late for us. Steve passed away from liver and kidney failure on April 28, 2002. At the tender age of thirty-two, he was gone, leaving his daughter, brothers, mother and friends to mourn him. I took his death incredibly hard, wanting to die myself.

Steve loved life, sometimes too much. I know he would have wanted me to continue living, enjoying life, not mourning him. And so I've been slowly healing in these years since his death, and regaining my zest for life.

It has taken twenty years for me to understand what I learned from Steve:

1. Love at first sight does exist, but keeping that love alive takes work.

2. Just because you've found your soul mate doesn't mean life will be perfect.

3. Addiction is a destroyer of relationships.

4. You don't stop loving someone just because they've hurt you. The love changes and carries pain with it, but it doesn't suddenly turn to indifference.

5. Moving on with life after the death of someone you love is hard, but you have to do it. Life is for the living.

6. You can love more than one person simultaneously. You have to commit your life and love to one person at a time, but you may still retain loving feelings for others, and you need to accept this and make it a positive in your life.

While I still think of Steve every so often, my life has moved past him. I now have a three-year-old daughter who's never met Steve, yet sometimes I swear she is familiar with him—his expressions, his facial movements, his spirit.

Could you play a song for Steve on July 10th? I know he still drops in on my life from time to time, to check on me. He always told me he would be watching over me, even when we broke up. I still love him, but my love has matured so I can accept this new way of having him in my life, and at thirty-six I know that the body doesn't last forever, but the spirit does.

Thank you,

Teresa

"Someone To Watch Over Me," performed by Patti Austin.
Songwriters: George Gershwin and Ira Gershwin.

"I WANT A HIPPOPOTAMUS FOR CHRISTMAS"

Dear Delilah,

"Marriage is hard work," my wife used to say. She died a few days ago, and suddenly marriage doesn't seem nearly as tough as losing a marriage partner. Kathleen was not only my wife but my soul mate, my sunrise and sunset, the grace that filled my soul and the wind under my wings. Our love continues even beyond the grave, and that's the story I want to share with you. You're even a part of the story!

You were her favorite media personality, and we went to bed with your radio show each night on WLIT in Chicago. During the Christmas season, WLIT plays Christmas music and each time "I Want a Hippopotamus for Christmas" came on, Kathleen would giggle and nudge me. "Listen, I love that song!" she would say. It reminded her of our six-year-old grandson, who's a great animal lover.

The year Kathleen died, 2007, was not a very good year for us. I had heart surgery with complications— my fingers and toes turned gangrenous and I was hospitalized for two months. Kathleen suddenly had to take over all the responsibilities. She had to clean the house, shovel the snow, talk to the doctors, visit me in the hospital, pay the bills, keep family and friends informed, and so forth. When I finally came home from the hospital, I was confined to a wheelchair and my hands and feet were charcoal-colored. I could not grip or walk. But Kathleen welcomed me as if my homecoming was the greatest thing that ever happened to her. She cared for me. She changed my wounds and soothed my sour spirit. She faced the impending amputations with courage and faith.

But then Kathleen herself was diagnosed with lung cancer. We vowed to fight it, and we tried. But in the end she died, and my heart broke. At her wake, as I knelt by her casket in the flower-filled chapel and said "Good night," I thought she seemed to be smiling.

She had not abandoned me—she was still with me.

I knew that couldn't be. I figured I was delusional from grief and exhaustion.

The day of her funeral, July 10th, one of Kathleen's oldest friends whispered to me to be sure to watch for Kathleen—watch, listen and smell. But I knew she was gone, and it was time to say goodbye. We began the funeral procession—sixty cars long and stretching for miles. My daughter was driving me right behind the hearse. She tried to comfort me, but could say nothing to make me feel better.

Then, as we followed the hearse into the cemetery

for the final farewell, it happened. My daughter noticed first. She had the car radio tuned to WLIT. And right in the middle of that hot summer day, WLIT was playing the song "I Want a Hippopotamus for Christmas." My daughter and I stared at each other wordlessly for a minute. Finally, we burst into tears—but tears of joy, not sadness. We knew Kathleen had sent us that song as a sign that she was happy. I could hear her giggle and I felt her nudge. She had not abandoned me—she was still with me.

Now there are cynics who chalk things like this up to coincidence. Well, I can't prove anything, Delilah, but I know that this was no coincidence. I believe my love did give a sign, and that she continues to hold my hand and whisper in my ear. I can smell her at times. I know I will see her again one day, and I know love can last forever. Please dedicate a song to the memory of my Kathleen.

Best regards to you, Delilah,

Frank

"I Want a Hippopotamus for Christmas," performed by Gayla Peevey. Songwriter: John Rox.

"If I Could Turn Back Time"

Dear Delilah,

I have so much to share but never do. I wanted to respond to a call/dedication I heard just now on the radio. It broke my heart and made me cry when I heard that story and then the song "Honesty." Someone had called you about a situation where the woman is planning on getting married but still has feelings for another. You gave the advice that she needs to be honest now so that there is no hurt down the road—you were so right, Delilah.

I love my husband dearly. . .and we now have two beautiful children. But twenty years ago, when I was a single college student, I met another man, and we seemed to be on the same wavelength. He lived far from me, so it wasn't feasible to pursue a relationship, but we worked together in the summer and talked on the phone a lot. Then, my senior year of college, he called and said "I'm getting married." I didn't say anything, but suddenly I knew I loved him and my heart was crushed. Still, I wanted him to be happy, so I bit my lip and quietly said, "Congratulations."

I did not go to the wedding. I went into a spiral of bad relationships. He still was there for me as a friend on the phone. Two years later, we ran into each other and got to talking. Somehow it came up about that devastating phone call, and he said that if I had told him that day, "I don't want you to get married" or "Wait!" he probably wouldn't have gotten married. That threw me into a horrible tailspin of "what-ifs," and I stayed away for another three years with only limited contact. I also met such a wonderful man (now my husband), who asked me to marry him. I said yes. I told my friend, and he said, "Well, now I know how you felt when I told you I was getting married." He came to my wedding. He cried and cried.

> We have always been able to be happy for each other in our lives as they are, but those feelings have continued to grow.

We are both Christians and have prayed that God would remove the feelings we have for each other. We have always been able to be happy for each other in our lives as they are, but those feelings have continued to grow. I just wanted to share this, with Delilah. I have not included my full name because it is the story that matters. I have come to terms with the fact that this love will never go away, but I will always regret that I was afraid to speak the truth when it mattered. I can only speak the whole truth now anonymously to you.

I would appreciate your letting me know if you do choose to read this on air or dedicate a song for me, so that I can be listening. Otherwise, just know that my heart and prayers are with you and your family and the families of those who care enough to share the loves and losses they have experienced.

Thank you very much!

Love,

Katie

"If I Could Turn Back Time," performed by Cher. Songwriter: Diane Warren.

"I Know You're Out There Somewhere"

Hello, Delilah,

I tried to save my marriage for the sake of our two daughters, but the marriage wasn't salvageable, and in the process I lost the man I have loved for eighteen years. With your help, I am hoping I can let him know that my heart still belongs to him and that I regret ever letting him go.

I met Kenneth when I was twenty-four and he was thirty-three. I was having lunch with my best friend at the navy base in Mayport, Florida, when he approached us. "Are you married?" he asked me, clearly interested.

Kenneth's ship left and my heart along with it.

At the time I was undergoing a nasty separation from my husband, who was in the navy, as Kenneth was. My husband was abusive and had cheated on me, but we were still legally married, so I looked down and said, "Yes." Then Kenneth placed his finger underneath my chin and gently raised my head back up. "Happily married?" he asked. I looked into his eyes and said, "No."

Well, Delilah, I couldn't deny the attraction, so I gave

Kenneth my phone number. We started dating and fell deeply in love with one another. I felt my heart had led me to this man. After we had been seeing each other for three months, Kenneth had to go out on a six-month deployment, and he told me he wanted to marry me when he came back. He asked me to promise I would be there for him when he returned, and I promised. He also warned me that my husband would try to convince me to return to him.

Kenneth's ship left and my heart along with it. As he had predicted, my husband tried to get me back. He had received orders to another port and begged me to give him another chance, for our family. I knew as I was leaving Florida that I was making the worst mistake of my life, but I felt that I had to try once more for my girls, ages two and four. That was in January 1990. We moved back to Virginia, and exactly three days later my husband and I got into an argument, and he got physically abusive in front of our daughters. I got a restraining order and then a divorce.

But meanwhile I had betrayed Kenneth. Although eventually he was able to forgive me, I wasn't able to forgive myself, and like a fool I threw away his phone number and had my own number changed. Why did I do that? I guess I had temporarily lost my mind after all the trauma of relocating, getting a job, finding child care and trying to find myself again. I told myself I was a mess and Kenneth would be better off without me. But, Delilah, I still love Kenneth, and there's an emptiness in my heart only he can fill. I have asked God to help me shake off my obsession with this man, but I can't seem to let go. I have moved back to Jacksonville, Florida, hoping that he will find me here. If it is not asking too much, could you please dedicate a song to Kenneth from Valerie? Maybe he will hear it or someone will pass it on to him.

Thank you so much for your message of Love, and the way you are there for people who call in or write to you. May God continue to richly bless and keep you in His special place.

Sincerely,
Valerie

"I Know You're Out There Somewhere," performed by Moody Blues. Songwriter: Justin Hayward.

"A Song for Mama"

Dear Delilah,

My daughter, Emily, age nine, listens to your show every night when she's going to sleep. Tonight I was helping her settle in for the night when you played a call from a listener asking for a dedication. The caller was a young gal, twenty-two, but her story was ripped from the pages of my life. Her mother passed away very recently, just shortly after this gal's son was born. She said how close she was to her mother, how they spoke every day, and you could hear the heartbreak in her voice.

You asked her how she is surviving, and she said her son keeps her going.

As I listened, I was transported back ten years, to the summer of '97, when I was

> I pray that I can be the kind of mom my mother was, because she was special.

thirty years old. I was living in California with my now-husband, pregnant with Emily, and preparing for my wedding when my mother, who was fifty-three, became ill very suddenly. Within two weeks she was gone—just twelve days before my husband and I were to be married.

My mother had been my very best friend. I was lucky that we remained close even when I went through the teenage years, while my friends were struggling with their relationships with their moms. I did struggle with my relationship with my father, and still do. But Mom and I had very few difficulties, for which I've always been grateful. The exception was when I got pregnant—initially that caused a rift between me and my mother, which was incredibly painful. But happily we got past that, and when my mom died, we were in the throes of wedding planning. Just days before she passed, I had sent her a box that contained items for my wedding day, including a photo of the dress I'd chosen. She saw the picture, but she never got to see me in the dress and she never got to see Emily—whose middle name is Jo, in honor of my mother.

When I listened to the story related tonight, it was one of those moments where all those very emotional feelings came rushing back. I am close to Emily, and I pray that we'll always remain close, as close as my mom and I were. And I also pray that I can be the kind of mom my mother was, because she was special.

I guess what I'd want that gal who called to know is that you do survive the loss. But you still miss your mother—I miss mine every day. I recently accepted a new job after several years of working in a difficult situation, and I wish she were here to talk to about it, and to celebrate with. I also know that losing Mom when I did contributed to who I am today. I am strong: I have been unable to have any more children due to a reproductive disorder, and after five miscarriages, I've accepted that Emily will be my only child. That wasn't easy to do. But I think losing a parent gives you the ability to cope with other losses.

Anyway, I just wanted you to know that your listener's story—and your compassionate response—touched someone deeply.

Very truly yours,
Karen

"A Song for Mama," performed by Boyz II Men.
Songwriters: Kenneth Edmonds aka Babyface.

"Live for Loving You"

Dear Delilah,

It truly is "better to have loved and lost than never to have loved at all." Let me tell you my story, and you can judge for yourself.

When I was twenty a doctor accidentally broke my water while performing an amniocentesis, and my daughter, Savannah, was born prematurely. Her birth weight was one pound, eight ounces, and she lived only sixteen days. I, too, had been close to death and was even given the last rites, but I survived. A year later, I became pregnant again, but it was a tubular pregnancy and I lost the baby. Then, six months after the miscarriage, I was diagnosed with stage-four cervical cancer and given a week to get my affairs in order and have surgery. I pulled through that also, but then three years afterward my whole world fell apart when my husband was killed in a shooting accident.

I swore I'd never love again—losing the ones I loved hurt too much—and I closed my heart or so I thought. In 2004 I met George, a wonderful man who changed

> Not to love is not to live.

everything. I could never have any more biological children because of the cancer, but George had kids and wanted me to be a part of his family. I wasn't sure his oldest daughter, Tina, would accept me, but as time passed, we became great friends. The day her dad and I got married, she threw her arms round me and said, "You've always been more of a mom to me than my own mom. I'm glad Dad married you and you're my mom." It was as if the big hole in my heart had finally been completely filled. But only three months later, Tina had a seizure in the middle of the night and passed away at age twenty-four.

The loss of Tina brought back the loss of Savannah, and once again I felt my heart was shattered. But this time I'm not closing off my heart. Rather, I'm reaching out in love to those who share my pain, including George and the beautiful daughter Tina left behind, who misses her, too. Please play a song for all of us. And I'd like to tell all those people out there who are saying to themselves, "I will never love again," that love is worth the pain, and not to love is not to live.

Love,

Lynn

"Live for Loving You," performed by Gloria Estefan.
Songwriters: Gloria Estefan, Emilio Estefan, Jr., Diane Warren.

"If You're Reading This"

Dear Delilah,

It's Christmas Eve and the kids are all asleep upstairs, or at least being quiet enough to hear Santa on the roof. They know not to open their bedroom doors lest the wonder and surprise be spoiled. Their mom and I are wrapping the last of the gifts and filling the stockings for Christmas morning. When first light breaks Christmas morning we'll be up, lighting the tree, starting the hot chocolate, making sure that Santa got everything right. Finally, when all is ready, five pairs of feet will come bounding down the stairs. Squeals of delight will meet each opened package and each goodie-crammed stocking.

This year the tradition continues, but with a major difference.

For the past sixteen years this has been the tradition in our family, whether at our home, in a hotel, or at friends' after a fire. The five pairs of feet have changed in number over the years as our kids dated and married, and now this year, we have our first grandchild. All are welcome to celebrate with us.

Yes, this year the tradition continues, but with a major difference. One of the original five will not be with us. Ryan was killed June 21, 2007, while serving in Baghdad on his second tour in Iraq. He was scheduled to be home for good on December 3, 2007. We are one of about four thousand families whose loved one will never be home again, and many thousands more are spending Christmas apart from loved ones serving around the world. Let us never forget them or the sacrifices they make.

Ryan's stocking is hung in its normal place; his ornaments are on the tree. The tradition will never change. We love you, son.

Delilah, please play a song in memory of Ryan, our joy, our hero, our son.

God bless,

Scott

"If You're Reading This," performed by Tim McGraw.
Songwriters: Tim McGraw, Brad Warren, Brett Warren.

"Live Like You Were Dying"

Dear Delilah,

I've just lost a dear friend, Tom, who died on August 22, 2007, just eight months after being diagnosed with advanced cancer. I've been close to Tom and his wife, Barb, for many years, and this is a terrible loss. Tom's spirit was stronger than a herd of elephants, but his body—despite four rounds of chemotherapy—couldn't keep fighting off the cancer.

I'm grateful for all the memories Tom left me. He and his wife used to volunteer with Northwest Medical Teams, and I remember helping them get ready for the last mission Tom was able to go on, to Moldova, Russia, on July 25th. I remember what a warm, sunny day it was, and how Tom insisted we weed the driveway together. There was a wonderful companionable silence as we worked together, sitting side by side on a gardening bench that we moved down the driveway each time we finished weeding a section.

Terrible as it is to lose a loved one, at least I was

At least I was able to say goodbye to Tom, a truly valuable gift.

able to say goodbye to Tom, a truly valuable gift. He was in hospice at the end, and Barb and I were visiting him together five days before he died. I sensed that he needed our permission to pass, and we gave it. He apologized for letting the cancer defeat him, but I told him he wasn't defeated at all—he had lived life to the fullest as long as he could, loved his wife and his friends and inspired all of us with his courage and devotion.

Delilah, please keep reminding your listeners to be mindful and present with the ones they love, whether family or friends. One final request—please dedicate a song as a memorial to my friend Tom.

Peace,

Kristi

"Live Like You Were Dying," performed by Tim McGraw.
Songwriters: Tim Nichols and Craig Wiseman.

Delilah fell in love with the airwaves as an eleven-year-old Girl Scout on a field trip to local radio station KDUN-AM in Reedsport, Oregon. At fourteen she had her first show, "Delilah on the Warpath," reporting school news and sports at the station, and by high school she was working at KDUN-AM six days a week. Today, over twenty-five years and fourteen stations later, Delilah's internationally syndicated show plays in more than 250 markets across North America. Airing from seven p.m. to midnight in most markets, she plays requests or finds the perfect song for callers who have an inspiring, heart-rending or simply amazing story to share with the beloved radio host and her more than 8 million devoted listeners.

A single mother of ten children, seven of them adopted, and a devoted grandmother, Delilah lives outside of Seattle, Washington, on forty-five acres of gardens and farmland. Because of her personal experience with the foster care system, Delilah has established the Point Hope Foundation as a voice for forgotten children. The immediate focus of Point Hope is on refugee children in Ghana and special needs children in foster care. Visit Delilah's Web site, www.delilah.com, and the Point Hope Web site, www.pointhope.org.